dangerous
desserts

dangerous
desserts

Edited by
Orlando Murrin

SOMA
san francisco

Contents

Text © The contributors 1998
Photography © The photographers 1998
(For a full list of contributors and photographers see page 172.)
Design & Layout © 1998 Quadrille Publishing Limited

First published in 1998 in the United Kingdom by BBC Books, an imprint of BBC Worldwide Ltd., London.

Designed and produced by Quadrille Publishing Limited, London

SOMA Books is an imprint of Bay Books & Tapes, Inc., 555 De Haro Street, No.220, San Francisco, CA 94107.

ISBN 1-57959-031-4

For the BBC Books edition:
Editor & Project Manager: Lewis Esson
Editorial Director: Jane O'Shea
Art Director: Mary Evans
Design: Paul Welti
Project Editor for the BBC: Jane Parsons
Production: Candida Jackson
Typesetting: Peter Howard

For the SOMA edition:
Publisher: James Connolly
Art Director: Jeffrey O'Rourke
Editorial Director: Clancy Drake
North American Editor: Beverley Le Blanc

Library of Congress Cataloging-in-Publication Data on file with publisher.

Printed and bound in Singapore by KHL Printing Co Pte Ltd

Introduction

No matter how sensible the rest of your food is, dessert is the time to give in to your wicked, wicked ways. This book has over 200 exquisite recipes and mouthwatering photos to guide you through a vast range of sweets and desserts—some so simple you can make them in seconds, others guaranteed to make your guests gasp in astonishment (and groan in pleasure).

These divinely dangerous desserts were written by a constellation of masterful pastry chefs from across Europe, and are presented here by noted food writer Orlando Murrin. Each of the eight chapters focuses on a different kind of dessert, from "Whipping up a Storm" (soufflés, mousses, and meringues), to "The Upper Crust" (tarts, pies, and pastries), to "Surrender to Chocolate" (well, you know). Every recipe is fully tested, clear, and user-friendly. In addition, most chapters are accompanied by a tremendously useful "master class"; a lesson in dessert classics—like crème brûlée and cheesecake—illustrated with full-color, step-by-step photographs.

So dive into a Glossy Chocolate and Peanut Butter Pie (page 87); indulge in Tiramisu Cheesecake (page 44); learn to make a perfect meringue (page 22); and cool your palate with Lemon Curd Ice Cream (page 146). Whether you are a novice cook or an experienced pastry chef, the recipes in this book will have you declaring, "If dessert is a crime, then let me be guilty!"

A slice from Phil Vickery's glorious Bitter Chocolate Pudding with Chocolate Fudge Sauce, see page 111.

Whipping Up a Storm

A seductive selection of soufflés, mousses, and meringues

Apple soufflés

Here the plain baked apple gets a makeover, to become a budding starlet.

Serves 6

9 large eating apples
1 tbsp. fresh lemon juice
4 tsp. butter
1 tsp. ground cinnamon
¼ cup superfine sugar
3 eggs, separated
confectioners' sugar for dusting

for the caramelized apples

3 tbsp. butter
¼ cup superfine sugar
1 tsp. finely grated lemon peel
1 tbsp. fresh lemon juice
2 tbsp. brandy or Calvados (optional)
light cream

1 Heat the oven to 375°F. Slice off the stalk end of 6 apples. Cut around the top edge of each apple and scoop out the flesh, leaving about a ½-inch border.

2 Brush all the cut edges of the apple cups with lemon juice to prevent discoloration. Roughly chop the flesh and place in a pan with 1 tablespoon water. Cover and cook 5 to 8 minutes until the apples are soft. Remove from the heat and press through a fine strainer into a bowl.

3 Beat the butter into the apple purée. Stir in the cinnamon, sugar, and egg yolks. In a clean, dry, greasefree bowl, beat the egg whites until stiff and dry. Using a large metal spoon, fold one-quarter into the apple mixture, then fold in the remainder, cutting through the mixture until evenly mixed.

4 Place the apple cups in a baking dish, using scrunched foil to keep them stable, if necessary. Carefully spoon in the soufflé mixture. Bake 20 to 25 minutes until well risen and golden brown.

5 Make the caramelized apples: Peel, core, and quarter the remaining apples; cut each quarter into 4 slices. Melt the butter in a skillet, add the apples, and cook quickly, turning once, until light golden. Stir in the sugar and lemon peel and juice and simmer a few minutes until syrupy. Keep warm until the soufflés are ready.

6 If using brandy or Calvados, add it to the caramelized apples, ignite carefully, and serve after the flames disappear. Place one apple soufflé on each warm serving plate with a small pile of the hot caramelized apples and some cream. Dust the soufflés with sifted confectioners' sugar and serve immediately.

Hot lemon soufflés

Sharp and sweet, these inexpensive little fruit cups make the most sophisticated last course.

Serves 6

1 tbsp. butter, plus more for the
   dish
8 large lemons
¾ cup plus 2 tbsp. superfine sugar
¾ cup plus 2 tbsp. milk
2 eggs, separated
1 tbsp. all-purpose flour
confectioners' sugar for dusting

1 Heat the oven to 400°F and butter a baking dish. Slice the tops off 6 of the lemons and scoop out the flesh and membranes. Strain this pulp through a fine nylon strainer; reserve the juice. Cut a thin slice off the bottom of each of the 6 lemons and stand them close together in the buttered dish.

2 Put the lemon juice and half of the sugar in a pan. Bring to a boil, stirring, until the sugar dissolves. Boil for 2 to 3 minutes until slightly syrupy. Stir in the butter and keep the sauce warm.

3 Pare the peel from one of the remaining lemons and place it in a pan with the milk. Heat slowly and simmer 2 minutes; remove the pared peel. Grate the peel from the last lemon; set aside.

4 Beat the egg yolks and half the remaining sugar until pale and thick. Beat in the flour, then strain in the milk. Bring the milk mixture slowly to a boil

in a pan, stirring until thick and smooth. Remove from the heat and stir in the grated lemon peel.

5 Beat the egg whites until foamy. Add the remaining sugar and beat until stiff. Fold into the custard mixture. Divide the mixture between the lemon shells. Bake 15 to 20 minutes until well risen and golden. Dust with sifted confectioners' sugar.

6 Pour the sauce onto 6 plates and quickly place the soufflés in the center of each. Serve at once.

Chocolate praline soufflé with marinated berries

The luxury of the best chocolate truffles in a melting soufflé, set off with mixed berries for an evening to remember.

Serves 4

for the praline
1/4 cup slivered almonds
7 tbsp. sugar

for the soufflé(s)
4 tsp. butter, cubed, plus more
   for the dish(es)
1/4 cup cornstarch
2/3 cup milk
6 1/2 tbsp. superfine sugar
1 tsp. vanilla extract
4 eggs, separated
2 3/4 ounces bitter chocolate, chopped

to serve
9 ounces mixed summer berries
2 tbsp. crème de cassis (optional)
confectioners' sugar for dusting

1 Heat the oven to 400°F. Make the praline: Line a baking sheet with foil. Toast the almonds in a dry skillet until golden brown. Put the sugar in a pan with 2 tablespoons cold water and heat slowly, stirring, until it dissolves. Without stirring, boil rapidly until the syrup turns the color of toffee. Immediately remove from the heat and stir in the toasted almonds. Pour onto the baking sheet and leave to cool about 15 minutes. Break into pieces. Reserve 8 nicely shaped pieces for decoration; process the rest in a food processor or blender until reduced to coarse crumbs.

2 Generously butter four 1 1/4-cup soufflé dishes or one 5-cup dish. In a pan, blend the cornstarch with 3 tablespoons of the milk. Stir in the remaining milk and the sugar. Cook over medium heat, stirring all the time, until the sauce thickens. Remove from the heat and stir in the butter, praline crumbs, vanilla, and egg yolks.

3 In a clean, dry, greasefree bowl, whisk the egg whites until stiff peaks form. Fold one-quarter of the egg whites into the sauce; then fold in the chocolate followed by the remaining egg whites.

4 Pour the mixture into the prepared dish(es) and set on a baking sheet. Bake 25 minutes for the small soufflés, or 30 to 35 minutes for the larger one until risen and golden brown.

5 Meanwhile, mix the berries with the cassis, if you are using. Remove the soufflé(s) from the oven and set on a plate or individual plates. Spoon the fruits around the soufflé(s) and decorate with the reserved praline pieces. Dust quickly with sifted confectioners' sugar and serve immediately.

Right: Made in teacups, ramekins and even scooped-out fruit, individual soufflés, like the Dark Mocha Soufflés, come in all guises.

Dark mocha soufflés with ice cream and mocha sauce

With the punch of strong coffee and the kick of brandy, these round off a dinner party perfectly.

Serves 6

butter for greasing
5 blanched almonds, finely ground
5 1/2 ounces semisweet chocolate
4 tbsp. strong black coffee
4 eggs, separated
2 tsp. all-purpose flour
1/2 cup superfine sugar
good-quality ice cream, to serve

for the mocha sauce
3 1/2 ounces semisweet chocolate
2/3 cup heavy cream
2 tbsp. strong black coffee
2 tbsp. brandy

1 Heat the oven to 375°F. Generously butter six 7-ounce ramekins or ovenproof teacups. Lightly dust the insides with the ground almonds.

2 Break the chocolate into a heatproof bowl and stir in the coffee. Set over a pan of simmering water and stir until it melts. Remove from the heat; leave to cool for a few minutes. Stir in the egg yolks, flour, and half the sugar.

3 Beat the egg whites in a clean, greasefree bowl. Beat in the remaining sugar, 1 tablespoon at a time. Using a large metal spoon, fold one-quarter of the egg whites into the chocolate sauce. Fold in the remainder, cutting through the mixture until evenly blended.

4 Divide the mixture between the prepared ramekins or teacups. Bake 20 to 25 minutes until well risen.

5 Make the sauce: Break the chocolate into a saucepan. Add the cream and coffee and stir over low heat until smooth and shiny. Stir in the brandy. Pour into a serving pitcher.

6 Serve the soufflés immediately. Each diner splits their soufflés, adds a scoop of ice cream, and pours some chocolate sauce over.

Master class: Making a soufflé

Candied fruit soufflés

Makes 4 to 6

2 tbsp. butter, softened

7 tbsp. sugar, plus more for the
  ramekins

1 cup mixed candied fruits, such as cherries,
  angelica, citrus peel, and apricots

4 tbsp. milk

1 vanilla bean, split, or ½ tsp. good-quality
  vanilla extract

4 tsp. honey

7 egg whites

8–12 vanilla-flavored macaroons (optional)

2 tbsp. confectioners' sugar

**for the crème pâtissière
(pastry cream)**

3 egg yolks

¼ cup superfine sugar

2½ tbsp. all-purpose flour

1 cup plus 2 tbsp. milk

1 vanilla bean, split, or 2 tsp. good-quality
  vanilla extract

butter or confectioners' sugar for cooling

1 Make the crème pâtissière: Beat the egg
yolks with about one-third of the sugar until
pale and of a light ribbon consistency. Sift the
flour over and beat thoroughly. In a saucepan,
bring the milk to a boil with the remaining
sugar and the vanilla bean or extract. As soon
as it begins to bubble, pour about one-third
onto the egg mixture, stirring continuously.
Pour this custard back into the pan and bring
to a boil over very low heat, stirring continuously. Bubble 2 minutes; transfer to a bowl.
Remove the vanilla bean, if using. Dot the
surface with a few flakes of butter or dust it
lightly with confectioners' sugar to prevent a
skin from forming as it cools.

These amounts makes about 1½ cups: the
remaining crème pâtissière not used in the
soufflé can be stored in the refrigerator for up
to 36 hours. Use it for pastries or cakes, or to
dress a fruit dessert.

2 Brush the insides of 4 to 6 individual
ramekins, which are 4 inches across and 2⅜
inches deep, with the softened butter. Put 2
tablespoons of the sugar into one dish and
rotate to coat the inside. Tip excess sugar into
the next dish (1); repeat to coat all the dishes.
Heat the oven to 425°F and place a baking
sheet in the oven to heat.

3 Assemble the soufflés: Chop the candied
fruit finely. Put the milk in a bowl and stir in
the candied fruit. Scrape out the inside of the
vanilla bean with the tip of a knife and stir it,
or the extract, into the milk. Place ¾ cup
crème pâtissière in a large bowl; if necessary,
warm it to tepid in a microwave oven or bain-
marie. Add the fruit mixture and honey.

4 Beat the egg whites until half risen (2); add
the remaining sugar and beat until stiff. Using
a balloon whisk, fold one-third of the egg
whites into the crème pâtissière (3). Add the
rest and fold in with a rubber spatula. Fill the
soufflé dishes one-third full with the mixture,
and sprinkle 2 lightly crushed macaroons over
each. Fill up the dishes and smooth the
surface with a metal spatula. Ease the mixture away from the edge of the dishes with the
tip of a knife (4).

5 Place the ramekins on the heated baking
sheet. Bake 6 to 7 minutes until well risen.

6 Dust each soufflé with a veil of sifted
confectioners' sugar, place on individual
plates, and serve at once.

Above: Chilled Valentine's Mousse made with white chocolate and decorated lovingly with cocoa powder hearts.

Left: Dark Chocolate Mousse in a Spiced Tuile Basket, served on a bed of raspberry sauce.

Chilled Valentine's mousses

For one large mousse, bake the cake in a flan ring, top with cherries, wrap in a paper collar, and spoon cream on top.

Serves 4

for the cake
1/2 cup plus 1 tbsp. superfine sugar
2 eggs, separated
1/4 cup unsweetened cocoa powder
3 tbsp. all-purpose flour
2 tbsp. kirsch (optional)

for the filling
14 ounces canned cherries, drained,
   or 1 pound fresh cherries, pitted

for the mousse
14 ounces bitter or white chocolate,
   broken into pieces
2 tbsp. dextrose
2 1/2 cups heavy cream
confectioners' sugar or unsweetened
   cocoa powder for dusting

1 Make the cake: Heat the oven to 325°F. Butter and line an 11 x 7-inch jelly-roll pan. Beat half of the sugar with the egg yolks until thick and pale. In a clean bowl, beat the egg whites until soft peaks form. Add the remaining sugar and beat to make a stiff meringue.
2 Sift the cocoa powder and flour into the egg yolk mixture; fold in. Beat in one-quarter of the meringue, then gently fold in the remaining meringue. Spread on the prepared pan to 1/4 to 1/2 inch thick. Bake 20 to 25 minutes until set. Leave to cool on a wire rack.
3 Using a plain cutter, cut out four 3-inch circles from the cake. Sit them in 3 1/2-inch ramekins; use leftover cake in a trifle. Sprinkle a little kirsch over if you like. If using canned cherries, place a few on top of each cake base. For fresh cherries, cook them in a little kirsch or water with sugar until tender. (If you don't want to use the liqueur, reserve the syrup from the cherries instead and

sprinkle it over the cake.) Set the ramekins aside.
4 Make the mousse: Melt the chocolate in a heatproof bowl set over warm water. Remove from the heat; let cool 5 minutes. Stir in the dextrose.
5 Whip the cream until it is just thick enough to hold its shape. Fold one-third into the melted chocolate; fold in the remaining cream. Tie strips of waxed paper around the ramekins to come 1 1/2 inches above the top; secure with tape. Spoon in the mousse so it comes roughly 1 inch above the ramekins. Smooth the tops and place in the refrigerator to set 1 to 2 hours for bitter chocolate and 3 to 4 if you are using white. Carefully remove the paper collars.
6 Cut a heart shape from a thin piece of cardboard. Hold the cardboard over the dessert and dust lightly with confectioners' sugar to make a heart. For a white chocolate dessert, make the heart by dusting with cocoa powder.

Dark chocolate mousse in a spiced tuile basket

This elegant presentation heralds a sophisticated flavor surprise. Serve with the raspberry sauce on page 94.

Serves 4

1 3/4 ounces white chocolate
raspberries and mint sprigs to garnish

for the chocolate mousse
6 ounces bitter chocolate
1 large egg yolk
1 tbsp. brandy
1 tbsp. butter, melted
1/2 cup heavy cream
2 large egg whites
1 tbsp. superfine sugar

for the spiced tuiles
2 tbsp. butter, plus extra for greasing
1/4 cup confectioners' sugar
1 small egg white
3 tbsp. all-purpose flour
1/4 tsp. each ground cinnamon, allspice,
   and cloves

1 Melt the white chocolate in a heatproof bowl set over a pan of simmering water. Place the chocolate in a waxed paper frosting bag. Pipe lacy "cobwebs" of chocolate on a baking tray lined with nonstick baking paper; chill until set.
2 Make the mousse: Melt the bitter chocolate in a heatproof bowl as above. Beat in the egg yolk, brandy, butter, and 3 tablespoons of the cream.
3 In a large bowl, whip the remaining cream until it holds its shape on the surface. Fold it into the chocolate mousse mixture.
4 In a separate bowl, beat the egg whites until soft peaks form. Gradually beat in the sugar and continue beating until stiff but not dry. Fold in the egg whites, a little at a time, until the chocolate mixture is combined. Spoon the mousse into a large pastry bag fitted with a star tip; set aside.
5 Make the tuiles: Heat the oven to 375°F. Line a

baking sheet with waxed paper and brush lightly with melted butter. In a bowl, beat the butter and confectioners' sugar together. Add the egg white and beat until smooth. Sift in the flour and spices and stir to make a smooth batter.
6 Spread the batter into four 4-inch circles about the thickness of a quarter on the baking sheet, well apart to allow for spreading. Bake 6 to 8 minutes until lightly browned. Leave to cool 1 minute or so. Using a metal spatula, carefully peel one from the baking sheet and shape it over an upturned cup. Repeat to make 3 more. Work quickly to shape them while they're still warm.
7 To serve, place a tuile basket on each plate. Pipe tall swirls of mousse into each basket and top with white chocolate "cobwebs." Decorate with raspberries, mint sprigs, and raspberry sauce.

Apricot, rosemary, and honey mousse

The wonderfully intense flavor of apricots in this creamy mousse is heightened by the delicate and unusual addition of fresh rosemary.

Serves 6

12 ounces fresh apricots
3 tbsp. honey
juice of 2 lemons
2 tsp. finely chopped fresh rosemary
    needles
1½ envelopes unflavored powdered
    gelatin
4 extra-large eggs, separated
pinch of salt
apricot slices and rosemary sprigs, to
    decorate

1 Halve the apricots, remove the pits, and chop the flesh into small pieces. Place in a saucepan with the honey, lemon juice, and rosemary. Bring to a boil, stirring continuously, until the honey melts. Lower the heat and simmer 15 to 20 minutes, stirring once or twice, until the apricots are reduced to pulp; set aside.
2 Sprinkle the gelatin over the hot apricot pulp and stir continuously for 2 minutes until it dissolves.
3 Bring a pan of water to a boil. Place the egg yolks in a heatproof bowl and set it over the pan. Stir the apricot mixture into the egg yolks and simmer about 5 minutes, stirring continuously, until the mixture thickens. Remove from the heat and leave the apricot mixture to cool.

4 Place the egg whites in a large bowl with the salt and beat until soft peaks form. Using a large metal spoon, fold the egg whites into the apricot mixture. Spoon into a large glass dish and chill at least 2 hours until set before serving.
5 Decorate with apricot slices and rosemary sprigs.

Right: Smooth sensuous Nectarine Mousse Cake, decorated with some halved strawberries and nectarine wedges, all glazed with apricot jam.

Nectarine mousse cake

Deceptively light, this is the ultimate in cream cakes, with a full fruit flavor.

Serves 6 to 8

for the cake layers
2 eggs
¼ cup superfine sugar
⅓ cup all-purpose flour
1 tbsp. unsweetened cocoa powder
for the mousse
6 ripe nectarines
1 tbsp. unflavored powdered gelatin
3 tbsp. fresh orange juice
4 to 5 tbsp. superfine sugar
1 egg white
⅔ cup heavy cream
to finish
seasonal fruit, to decorate
2 tbsp. apricot jam, to glaze
loganberry sauce, to serve (optional)

1 Heat the oven to 400°F. Grease and line a baking sheet with waxed paper. Mark two 8-inch circles on the paper. Beat together the eggs and sugar 10 minutes until the mixture is thick and pale and leaves a trail when the beaters are lifted. Sift the flour over and fold it in. Transfer half the batter to a separate bowl and sift in the cocoa powder; fold it in. Place alternate spoonfuls of the batter on the marked circles, spreading it to the edges. Swirl the batter together with a skewer. Bake 10 to 12 minutes until the cakes are firm. Remove the lining paper and leave to cool on a wire rack.
2 Line a 7-inch round cake pan with plastic wrap. Using a sharp knife, trim the cake circles to fit the pan.
3 Make the mousse: Skin, pit, and purée the

nectarines. Dissolve the gelatin in the orange juice in a small bowl set over a pan of hot water. Stir into the nectarine purée with the sugar. Beat the egg white and whip the cream. Using a large metal spoon, fold the egg white and cream into the purée.
4 Line the bottom of the cake pan with one of the cake circles. Pour in the mousse and cover with the other cake circle. Chill several hours until set.
5 Turn out and decorate with fresh fruit. Warm the jam and push through a fine strainer; brush over the fruit. Serve with loganberry sauce, if you like.

White and dark chocolate mousse

This easy-to-make, black-and-white marbled mousse makes the most elegant party dessert.

Serves 6 to 8

butter for the pan
6 ounces Madeira cake or pound
    cake
2 tbsp. brandy
1 tbsp. cold, strong black coffee
6 ounces semisweet chocolate,
    broken into pieces
6 ounces white chocolate, broken
    into pieces
2 cups heavy cream

1 Grease an 8-inch springform cake pan and line the bottom with nonstick baking paper. Line the sides with strips of foil. Slice the cake and use it to line the bottom of the cake pan, cutting the pieces to fit. Mix the brandy with the coffee and drizzle this over the cake.

2 Melt both types of chocolate in separate heatproof bowls over pans of hot water. Whip the cream until it holds its shape; divide it between 2 bowls. Stir the semisweet chocolate into one bowl and the white chocolate into the other.

3 Spoon alternating blobs of white and semisweet chocolate mixtures over the cake and, using a skewer, swirl them into one another. Smooth the surface and chill for at least 2 hours until set.

4 Remove the mousse from the cake pan and peel off the foil. Place the mousse on a serving plate and chill again until ready to serve.

Variation:
Instead of the coffee and brandy, flavor this mousse with an orange-flavored liqueur.

Strawberry mousses

Serve these as the finale to an alfresco summer lunch—or even for a picnic.

Makes 8

12 ounces strawberries, hulled
5 tsp. unflavored powdered gelatin
2 eggs, separated
2 tbsp. cornstarch
2/3 cup heavy cream
2/3 cup milk
1/2 cup superfine sugar
extra strawberries, to decorate

1 Purée the strawberries in a food processor or blender.

2 In a small bowl, sprinkle the gelatin over 3 tablespoons cold water. (Never pour water over gelatin or it will set solid!) Leave to soak.

3 Place the egg yolks in a pan with the cornstarch and stir until smooth. Gradually stir in the cream, milk, and sugar. Bring to a boil, stirring constantly, until the mixture becomes thick and smooth. Stir in the softened gelatin. Beat in the strawberry purée.

4 In a clean, dry, greasefree bowl, beat the egg whites until soft peaks form. Using a spatula, beat one-quarter of the egg whites into the strawberry mixture; fold in the remainder.

5 Spoon into 8 individual molds or ramekins, or one large dish. Chill several hours until set.

6 To unmold, loosen the edges of the mousses carefully with a knife. Dip briefly in very hot water and invert onto a serving plate. Decorate with strawberries.

Chocolate marquise slice

This substantial layered chocolate terrine makes an impressive buffet table centerpiece.

Serves 8

1 cup chopped pitted prunes
3 tbsp. brandy
1 tbsp. unflavored powdered gelatin
7 ounces semisweet chocolate,
 broken into pieces
5 ounces white chocolate, broken
 into pieces
4 tbsp. milk
1 cup heavy cream
2 tbsp. unsweetened cocoa powder
6 egg whites
½ cup superfine sugar

for the ribbons

3½ ounces semisweet chocolate

1 Line a 9 x 5-inch bread pan with plastic wrap so it fits into the corners and hangs over the edges. Place the prunes in the brandy to soak. Sprinkle half the gelatin over 2 tablespoons cold water in a bowl; repeat the process in another bowl with the remaining gelatin.

2 Melt the 2 chocolates in separate bowls, each with half the milk. Stir half the cream into each bowl until smooth; add the cocoa powder to the bittersweet chocolate.

3 Place each bowl of gelatin over a pan containing a little simmering water until the gelatin dissolves. Beat one mixture into the semisweet chocolate, the other into the white chocolate.

4 Put the egg whites and sugar in a large bowl; sit this over a pan of simmering water. Beat with an electric mixer for 5 minutes until it forms a stiff, glossy meringue.

5 Spoon half the meringue into another bowl; fold the semisweet chocolate into it. Repeat with the white chocolate and prunes with their soaking liquid. Leave until the mixtures are beginning to set.

6 Spoon half the semisweet chocolate into the bottom of the prepared bread pan. Add half the white; repeat the layers.

7 Freeze for several hours until firm.

8 Make the chocolate ribbons: Melt the chocolate. Cut out ten 6 x 2-inch rectangles of stiff, clear plastic. Spread a little melted chocolate on one rectangle, swirling it decoratively near the edges with the tip of a spoon. Bring 2 short ends together, with the chocolate inside, to form a ring; secure the plastic with tape. Repeat and leave to set. Hold the ends of the plastic together so the chocolate doesn't crack, cut the tape, and remove gently.

9 Turn out the marquise, cut it into thick slices, and decorate with the chocolate ribbons.

Master class: Making Pavlova

Fruit Pavlova

Pavlova was created in honor of Anna Pavlova, the Russian prima ballerina, when she visited Australia and New Zealand in the 1920s. The perfect Pavlova is crisp on the outside and yet soft—almost marshmallowlike—on the inside.

Serves 6

butter for greasing
4 egg whites
1 cup plus 2 tbsp. sugar
1 tsp. white-wine vinegar
1 tsp. cornstarch

for the filling

¾ cup heavy cream
1 tbsp. confectioners' sugar
1 tbsp. Marsala or dry sherry (optional)
1 cup plus 2 tbsp. mascarpone cheese
3 to 4 ounces strawberries
3 to 4 ounces raspberries
1 ripe peach, sliced

1 Heat the oven to 275°F. Lightly grease a baking tray and line it with nonstick baking paper. Using a plate as a guide, draw a 9-inch circle on the paper.

2 In a large, clean, dry bowl, beat the egg whites until stiff peaks form.

3 Gradually beat in the sugar, 1 tablespoon at a time, until the meringue becomes thick and glossy. Fold in the white-wine vinegar and cornstarch.

4 Spoon half the mixture onto the baking paper to fill the circle. Drop large spoonfuls of the remaining mixture on top, adding more to the edges to form a high rim.

5 Place the meringue in the center of the oven. After 5 minutes, lower the temperature to 250°F. Bake 50 minutes; turn the oven off without opening the door. Leave the meringue in the oven at least 3 hours or overnight to cool completely. Transfer to a wire rack and remove the baking paper. Place on a large serving plate.

6 Make the filling: Whip the cream with the sugar; fold in the Marsala or sherry, if using, and the mascarpone. Spoon into the meringue case and pile the fruit on top. Keep cool, but do not refrigerate, before serving.

Top tips for meringues

* Set the temperature of the oven very low so the meringue cooks slowly and remains white.
* Beat the egg whites in a spotlessly clean bowl; the slightest trace of grease will prevent them from beating to full volume.
* The egg whites must be firmly beaten between additions of sugar. If you rush this stage, a syrupy liquid can separate out during baking.
* The addition of white-wine vinegar (or lemon juice) and cornstarch makes sure the meringue turns out soft and fluffy inside.

Flavoring meringues

To give meringue a special flavor, carefully fold in the following when preparing the meringue mixture, before shaping and baking:
* coarsely grated chocolate—it melts lusciously into the meringue as it bakes.
* ground or coarsely chopped hazelnuts, almond, or other nuts—toast them before use to give a wonderful taste and texture to the meringue.
* finely grated orange and/or lemon peel—it gives the meringue a zing.

Meringue peaches

Give canned fruit this luxury treatment for a dessert to remember.

Makes 4

14 ounces canned peach halves,
   drained
8 amaretti cookies, macaroons, or
   any other small, crunchy cookies
2 to 3 tablespoons orange-flavored
   liqueur
1 egg white
¼ cup superfine sugar
¼ cup slivered almonds
confectioners' sugar for dusting
4 Cape gooseberries, to decorate
   (optional)

1 Heat the oven to 400°F. Pat the peaches dry with paper towels. Place hollow side up on a baking sheet. Place one amaretti cookie inside each hollow and drizzle the liqueur over.
2 Beat the egg white in a bowl until stiff. Gradually beat in the sugar until it is glossy.
3 Fill a pastry bag fitted with a star-shaped tip with the meringue. Pipe the meringue in a swirl over each peach.
4 Sprinkle the almonds over. Bake about 10 minutes, or until the meringue is a pale golden brown.
5 Lightly dust the meringues with the sifted confectioners' sugar. Serve on individual plates, decorated with the Cape gooseberries.

Passion fruit islands

Custard flavored with exotic passion fruit is molded into heart shapes and dressed with caramel.

Makes 2

for the custard
5 passion fruit
3 egg yolks
5 tbsp. superfine sugar
2 tsp. cornstarch
2 cups milk
2 tbsp. orange-flavored liqueur
   (optional)
for the caramel
¼ cup superfine sugar
for the meringue
1 egg white
2 tbsp. superfine sugar
1¼ cups milk

1 Make the custard: Cut 4 passion fruit in half and press the pulp through a strainer to extract the juice; reserve the juice. Beat together the egg yolks, sugar, and cornstarch until pale and creamy.
2 In a saucepan, bring the milk to a boil. Pour it into the egg mixture. Return the mixture to the pan and simmer over low heat, stirring, about 15 minutes until thick; do not let boil. Remove from the heat and cover the surface with waxed paper to prevent a skin from forming; leave to cool.
3 When cool, stir in the passion fruit juice and the liqueur, if using. Pour the custard into 2 shallow serving dishes.
4 Make the caramel: Wrap a piece of waxed paper around a rolling pin. Heat the sugar in a small, heavy-bottomed pan with 3 tablespoons water until it dissolves. Bring to a boil and boil rapidly until the syrup turns deep golden. Immerse the bottom of the pan in cold water to stop the

cooking. Using a teaspoon, drizzle the caramel in streaks over the rolling pin. If the caramel runs off the pin, leave it to cool for 30 seconds; leave to set.
5 Make the meringue: Beat the egg white until stiff. Gradually beat in the sugar, a little at a time, until the meringue is stiff and glossy.
6 In a small skillet, bring the milk to a low simmer. Place a large, heart-shaped cookie cutter on a sheet of waxed paper; fill with about a quarter of the meringue. Peel away the paper and cook the meringue in the milk for 1 minute. Flip the cutter over and cook 1 minute longer. Drain the meringue and lift away the cutter. Make 3 more hearts in the same way.
7 Cut the remaining passion fruit into quarters. Place the custards on serving plates and place 2 meringues on top of each. Arrange caramel pieces on top and decorate with passion fruit quarters.

Cherry and almond queen of puddings

This pantry dessert will impress unexpected guests, making it a good last-minute family treat.

Serves 6

2 tbsp. butter
³⁄₄ cup fresh bread crumbs
20 blanched almonds, finely ground
finely grated peel of 1 lemon
³⁄₄ cup plus 2 tbsp. sugar
1¹⁄₄ cups light cream
1¹⁄₄ cups milk
1 tsp. almond extract
3 large eggs, separated
1¹⁄₂ pounds bottled pitted red cherries
4 tsp. cornstarch
finely ground blanched almonds for
   sprinkling

1 Heat the oven to 350°F. Lightly butter a 6¹⁄₄-cup deep, oval baking dish. Mix the bread crumbs, almonds, lemon peel, and 2 tablespoons superfine sugar in a bowl.

2 In a saucepan, heat the remaining butter, cream, milk, and almond extract, stirring until the butter melts. Pour over the bread crumb mixture; set aside 10 minutes. Beat in the egg yolks. Pour into the prepared dish. Bake 20 minutes until lightly set.

3 In a pan, blend 4 tablespoons cherry juice with the cornstarch. Stir in another ²⁄₃ cup of the juice and simmer, stirring, 3 to 4 minutes. Drain the cherries and add to the pan. Spoon over the custard.

4 Increase the oven temperature to 400°F. Beat the egg whites until stiff. Gradually add the

remaining sugar, beating well after each addition. Spoon the meringue over the cherries and sprinkle with ground almonds. Bake 8 to 10 minutes longer, until lightly browned.

Left: Halving the strawberries before arranging them makes it easier to serve such a dramatically appealing portion of Mississippi Meringue Pie.

Mississippi meringue pie

Fresh strawberries and a meringue topping turn this simple refrigerator cake into a Southern belle.

Serves 12

1 stick plus 1 tbsp. butter
3 tbsp. chocolate-hazelnut spread
2¹⁄₂ cups crushed chocolate-covered
   graham cracker crumbs
for the filling
1 tbsp. unflavored powdered gelatin
1¹⁄₄ cups superfine sugar
2 tbsp. cornstarch
3 large eggs, separated
2 cups light cream
1 tbsp. instant coffee granules
7 ounces semisweet chocolate
²⁄₃ cup heavy cream, whipped
1¹⁄₂ pounds strawberries, hulled

1 In a large pan, slowly melt the butter and chocolate spread. Stir in the crumbs and mix well. Press the mixture into the bottom and sides of a deep 8-inch fluted loose-bottomed tart pan; chill until ready to use.

2 Sprinkle the gelatin over 6 tablespoons warm water in a small bowl; leave to soak 5 minutes. In another small bowl, mix one-third of the sugar with the cornstarch, egg yolks, and a little of the light cream to make a smooth paste. In a pan, heat the remaining light cream with the coffee and chocolate, broken in pieces, until the chocolate melts. Stir in the cornstarch mixture and simmer, stirring until the custard thickens enough to coat the back of a wooden spoon.

3 Set the gelatin mixture over a pan of simmering

water and heat until it dissolves. Stir into the hot custard; leave to cool slightly. Fold in the whipped cream. Pour the mixture into the crumb case; chill until set.

4 Heat the broiler to hot. Beat the egg whites until stiff. Gradually beat in the remaining sugar until the meringue is thick and glossy. Arrange the strawberries over the chocolate filling. Spoon the meringue over to cover. Broil for 3 to 4 minutes until browned.

Hazelnut, banana, and caramel nests

This dessert is a lesson in how to put on a show with the simplest ingredients.

Makes 4

for the meringue
2 egg whites
½ cup superfine sugar
¼ tsp. white-wine vinegar
¼ tsp. cornstarch
2 tbsp. hazelnuts, toasted and finely
  chopped

for the filling
3 ripe bananas, roughly chopped
1 tbsp. lemon juice
2 tbsp. maple syrup
½ cup thick plain yogurt

for the caramel topping
¼ cup superfine sugar

1 Heat the oven to 250°F. Line a baking sheet with nonstick baking paper.
2 In a large, clean, dry, greasefree bowl, beat the egg whites until stiff peaks form. Gradually beat in the sugar, 1 tablespoon at a time, until the meringue is thick and glossy. Fold in the white-wine vinegar and cornstarch, followed by the toasted hazelnuts.
3 Fill a pastry bag fitted with a ½-inch plain tip with the meringue. Pipe four 4-inch circles on the paper. Pipe another line of meringue around the edge of the circles to create nests.
4 Bake for 1 hour until the meringue nests are crisp. Remove from the paper and leave to cool on a wire rack.
5 Make the filling: Toss the bananas with the lemon juice. Stir them and the maple syrup into the yogurt. Spoon into the middle of each nest.
6 Make the caramel topping: Place the sugar in a small saucepan and heat slowly until it starts to melt; swirl the pan around so the sugar melts evenly. Continue simmering until the syrup has a light caramel color. Remove the pan from the heat; leave to stand for a few minutes.
7 Line a baking sheet with nonstick baking

paper. Using a tablespoon, trail thin threads of the caramel over the paper in a crisscross pattern; continue until all the caramel is used. Leave to cool until crisp. Peel the paper away

from the caramel and use it to decorate the top of each basket. Serve immediately.

Saffron meringues with lemon syllabub

Spice up your meringues with the magical flavor and color of saffron.

Makes 6

pinch of saffron strands
2 egg whites
1/2 cup superfine sugar
1/4 tsp. white-wine vinegar
1/4 tsp. cornstarch
for the lemon syllabub
grated peel and juice of 1/2 lemon
2 tbsp. dry sherry
2 tbsp. superfine sugar
2/3 cup heavy cream

1 Heat the oven to 250°F. Line a baking sheet with nonstick baking paper. Place the saffron strands in a small bowl, pour 1 tablespoon boiling water over them, and leave to infuse.
2 In a large, clean, dry, greasefree bowl, beat the egg whites until stiff peaks form. Gradually beat in the sugar, 1 tablespoon at a time, until the meringue becomes thick and glossy. Fold in the white-wine vinegar and cornstarch.
3 Drain the saffron. Fold the soaked strands into the meringue to create a streaked effect; be careful not to overwhip.
4 Using 2 tablespoons, shape the meringue into 12 oval mounds on the prepared baking sheet.

Bake 1 hour until crisp on the outside and chewy inside. Turn off the oven and leave the meringues to cool in the oven 1 hour.
5 Make the lemon syllabub: Place the lemon juice and peel and the sherry in a large bowl and stir in the sugar until it dissolves. Stir in the cream and beat 4 to 5 minutes until soft peaks form; chill until required.
6 Sandwich pairs of meringue ovals with the syllabub filling. Serve immediately.

The caramel topping for the Hazelnut, Banana, and Caramel Nest opposite can be used to give a touch of grandeur to the simplest of desserts, even a dish of plain fruit.

Exotic fruit layer (See the picture on page 8)

The creamy exotic fruit filling and cardamom-flavored meringue make this a fitting finale to a spicy meal.

Makes 6

3 egg whites
3/4 cup plus 2 tbsp. superfine sugar
1 tsp. lemon juice
1 tsp. cornstarch
1 tbsp. crushed cardamom seeds, pods removed
for the filling
1 1/4 cups heavy cream, lightly whipped
1 papaya, roughly chopped
1 mango, roughly chopped
2 passion fruit
coconut flakes, toasted, to decorate

1 Heat the oven to 300°F. Line 2 baking sheets with nonstick baking paper. Draw three 4 1/2 x 9-inch rectangles on the paper; 2 on one, 1 on the other.
2 In a large, clean, dry, greasefree bowl, beat the egg whites until stiff peaks form. Gradually beat in the sugar, 1 tablespoon at a time, until the meringue becomes thick and glossy. Fold in the lemon juice and cornstarch, followed by the cardamom seeds.
3 Spoon the meringue onto the rectangles on the prepared baking sheets and spread out evenly. Place in the oven and lower the setting to 275°F. Bake for 1 hour. Turn off the oven and leave the meringues in the oven until cold.
4 Remove the meringues from the baking sheets

and peel off the paper. Arrange one meringue rectangle on a serving plate and spoon half the cream on top. Sandwich a second meringue rectangle on top, followed by a layer of half the fruits and the remaining cream. Place the final meringue rectangle on top and top with the remaining fruits. Scatter the coconut flakes over. Cut into slices and serve immediately.

Variation:
Instead of cardamom, flavor the meringue with saffron as in the recipe above, or 2 teaspoons finely chopped candied ginger.

Meringue Christmas tree

Season's beatings for this original edible table decoration.

Serves 6 to 8

4 egg whites
2¼ cups confectioners' sugar, sifted
1¼ cups heavy cream
1¼ cups thick plain yogurt

for decoration

1 star fruit
2 clementines or tangerines
½ cup superfine sugar
3 to 4 ounces small seedless green or
    red grapes
a few cranberries (optional)

1 Heat the oven to 250°F. Line 3 baking sheets with nonstick baking paper. Mark circles on the paper with the following diameters: 2 inches, 3 inches, 4 inches, 5 inches, 6 inches, 7 inches.
2 Place the egg whites and confectioners' sugar in a large, clean, dry, greasefree bowl set over a pan of simmering water. Using an electric mixer, beat 10 minutes until the mixture is stiff and soft peaks form.
3 Remove the bowl from the heat and continue beating 2 to 3 minutes. Spoon the meringue over the marked circles on the baking sheets, shaping the edges into curves. Peak the center of the smallest meringue and the edges of the remaining ones.
4 Bake the meringues 1½ hours until pale golden. Turn off the oven and leave the meringues in the oven to finish baking in the residual heat.
5 Prepare the decoration: Slice the star fruit and segment the clementines. Heat half of the sugar in a small pan with 2 tablespoons water until the sugar dissolves. Increase the heat, then boil rapidly 2 to 3 minutes until the syrup turns a golden caramel.
6 Remove the pan from the heat and leave until

the bubbles subside. Spear the clementines, grapes, and cranberries, if using them, on a fork; dip them into the caramel to coat. Transfer to a sheet of foil to set. Continue until all of the fruit is coated; do not coat the star fruit.
7 Whip the cream until stiff; fold in the yogurt. Reserve one small slice of star fruit. Set the largest meringue on a plate and spread with a little cream. Arrange some of the fruit over the cream and cover with the next largest meringue circle. Continue layering the meringue, cream, and fruit, finishing with the smallest meringue.
8 Just before serving, place the remaining sugar in a small, clean pan with 2 tablespoons water; make a caramel as before. Let cool 5 minutes. Stick the reserved star fruit onto the top of the cake with a little of the caramel. Using a metal spoon, lift a little more caramel out of the pan, dip the back of a fork into this and pull up quickly to form strands. Wrap these quickly around the "tree." Repeat until all the caramel is used and the tree is evenly covered in strands.
9 Serve within 1 hour. The undecorated meringues will keep in an airtight container for up to a week.

Red currant meringue roulade

The sweet-sourness of the red currants and the yogurt gives this roulade a sophisticated edge.

Serves 8

3 egg whites
1 tsp. vanilla extract
1 tsp. cornstarch
1 tsp. white-wine vinegar
1 cup plus 2 tbsp. superfine sugar
2 tbsp. finely chopped toasted
    hazelnuts
6 ounces red currants
⅔ cup heavy cream
⅔ cup thick plain yogurt

1 Heat the oven to 275°F. Line a shallow 13 x 9-inch cake pan with waxed paper.
2 Beat the egg whites in a clean, dry, greasefree bowl until stiff. Stir together the vanilla extract, cornstarch, and vinegar. Beat ¾ cup plus 2 tablespoons of the sugar into the egg whites, 1 tablespoon at a time, adding a little of the vanilla mixture with each addition. Beat the mixture until it is stiff and marshmallowlike.
3 Spread the mixture over the prepared cake pan and sprinkle with the nuts. Bake 40 minutes. Remove the pan from the oven and cover the

meringue with foil.
4 Place the red currants, the remaining sugar, and 1 tablespoon of water in a pan and simmer about 5 minutes until softened. Press through a fine strainer; leave to cool. Beat the cream until stiff, then fold in the yogurt.
5 Turn the meringue out on a sheet of waxed paper. Spread with the cream mixture, then the red currant purée. Using the paper to help you, roll up the meringue from one short end. Transfer to a serving plate. Chill for up to 2 hours before serving.

Hazelnut meringue roulade with mango and orange cream

The citrus zing of oranges brings out the best of the mango flavor for this memorable special-occasion dessert.

Serves 6 to 8

¾ cup shelled hazelnuts
1 tsp. cornstarch
1 tsp. vanilla extract
1 tsp. white-wine vinegar
4 extra-large egg whites
¾ cup superfine sugar
confectioners' sugar for dusting

for the filling
1 large or 2 medium ripe mangoes
2 tbsp. sugar
1 tsp. finely grated orange peel
¾ cup plus 2 tbsp. crème fraîche or
  sour cream

for the sauce
1 large ripe mango
2 tbsp. sugar
4 to 6 tbsp. orange juice

1 Heat the oven to 325°F. Line a shallow 13 x 7-inch cake pan with a sheet of nonstick baking paper, snipping corners to fit.
2 Toast the hazelnuts in a small, dry skillet until light golden flecked with brown. Tip into a food processor and grind to a fine powder.
3 Blend together the cornstarch, vanilla, and vinegar to a smooth paste. Beat the egg whites in a clean, dry bowl until stiff peaks form. Beat in the sugar, a little at a time, adding a little of the cornstarch mixture each time until all the sugar and paste is added. The meringue will be thick, very white, and stiff.
4 Reserve 2 tablespoons of the ground hazelnuts, then, using a large metal spoon, fold the remainder into the meringue until just mixed.
5 Spoon the meringue into the prepared cake pan and level the surface with the back of a spoon; don't worry about making it too smooth because the craggy texture makes a charming crust when baked. Sprinkle with the reserved hazelnuts.

6 Bake about 25 minutes until the meringue is pale golden on top and feels crisp and dry when lightly touched. Lay a sheet of baking paper on the counter, remove the meringue from the oven, and turn it out on the paper. Peel off the lining paper and leave the meringue to cool uncovered; it will sink slightly.
7 Make the filling: Halve the mango each side of the pit, peel, and pit. Chop the flesh into small cubes. Mix in a bowl with the sugar and orange peel. Fold in the crème fraîche.
8 Spread the filling over the meringue to within ½ inch of the edges. Roll up from one short end, using the paper to help you; the meringue will crack slightly as it is rolled. Transfer to a serving plate and dust with sifted confectioners' sugar.
9 Make the sauce: Peel, halve, and pit the mango. Chop off the flesh and process in a food processor with the sugar and orange juice. Press through a strainer if necessary. Serve with the slices of roulade.

Tarte aux groseilles meringuée

You can make this delicious tart with any firm berry fruit—try blueberries for a change.

Serves 6

for the pastry dough
1⅓ cups all-purpose flour
pinch of salt
½ cup superfine sugar
7 tbsp. unsalted butter
2 eggs, beaten

for the filling
1 cup slivered almonds
½ tsp. finely grated lemon peel
2 tbsp. red-currant jelly
⅔ cup blanched almonds, finely
  ground
1 cup superfine sugar
1 pound red currants
5 egg whites
1 tbsp. confectioners' sugar

1 Make the dough: Sift the flour, salt, and sugar in a thick layer onto a large chopping board or clean countertop. Cut the butter into small pieces and dot these on top. Cut the butter into the flour and sugar to form fine crumbs. Make a well in the middle, pour in the eggs, and draw them into the mixture with your fingers to form a soft dough. Knead gently and shape into a ball. Wrap in plastic wrap; chill 30 minutes.
2 Heat the oven to 400°F. Roll out the dough on a lightly floured surface and place in a loose-bottomed 12-inch tart pan. Line the dough with foil and dried beans. Bake 15 minutes. Remove the beans and foil and bake 5 minutes longer. Remove from the oven and leave to cool on a wire rack.
3 Lower the oven temperature to 350°F. In a dry, nonstick skillet, toast the almonds until pale

golden. Stir in the lemon peel and red-currant jelly. Spread the mixture evenly over the tart case.
4 Sift the ground almonds and half the sugar into a bowl. Strip the red currants from their stems and lightly coat in the almond mixture. Arrange the red currants in the tart case; set aside the remaining sweetened almonds.
5 In a clean, dry, greasefree bowl, beat the egg whites until stiff peaks form. Sift the remaining sugar with the reserved sweetened ground almonds. Gradually beat into the egg whites, 1 tablespoon at a time, until the meringue is thick and glossy. Spoon the meringue over the red currants. Bake 25 to 30 minutes, or until the top is pale golden and set.
6 Serve dusted with confectioners' sugar.

More than mere trifles

The smooth charms of custards, creams, and gelatin molds

Cranberry, pear, and chocolate trifle with pear crisps

The combination of tart berries, semisweet and white chocolates, pears, and whiskey turn this into a grown-up dessert.

Serves 8

6 ripe pears
8 tbsp. whiskey
¾ cup superfine sugar
1 pound cranberries, thawed if
    frozen
9 ounces chocolate cake, cut into
    ½-inch slices
2 ounces good-quality semisweet
    chocolate, chopped, to decorate
**for the white chocolate
custard**
5 ounces good-quality white
    chocolate, chopped
1¾ cups freshly made custard sauce
    (see page 40)
1¼ cups heavy cream
for the pear crisps
2 ripe pears
½ cup sugar

1 Prepare the pear crisps: Heat the oven to 250°F. Line a nonstick baking sheet with nonstick baking paper. Without peeling or coring, slice 2 pears very thinly from top to bottom. In a skillet, dissolve the sugar in 7 tablespoons water over medium heat. Bring to a boil, then simmer 2 to 3 minutes. Remove from the heat, add the pear slices, and leave 2 minutes. Remove with a spatula and place on a baking sheet. Bake 1½ hours until just golden. Cool on a wire rack.
2 Meanwhile, peel, core, and quarter the remaining 6 pears. Heat 2½ cups water with 2 tablespoons of the whiskey and ½ cup of the sugar in a large pan, stirring, until the sugar dissolves. Add the pears and simmer 7 to 8 minutes until just tender. Drain; set aside to cool.
3 In a pan, over low heat, simmer the cranberries and the remaining ¼ cup sugar until the berries start to soften. Drain a spoonful on paper towels; reserve for decoration. Set the rest aside to cool.
4 Layer half the cake in the bottom of a glass

serving dish. Sprinkle with half the remaining whiskey. Arrange half the pear quarters on top and cover with half the cranberries; repeat layers.
5 Make the white chocolate custard: Melt the white chocolate in a heatproof bowl set over a pan of simmering water; do not let the bowl touch the water. Remove from the heat and leave to cool. Pour the custard into a large bowl and stir in the melted chocolate. Lightly whip the cream and fold into mixture. Pour over the trifle. Chill until set.
6 To decorate, stand the pear crisps in the top of the trifle. Sprinkle the reserved cranberries and chopped semisweet chocolate over.

(See the picture on page 34)

Mascarpone and rum trifle

The mascarpone cheese gives this trifle the creamy texture of a cheesecake.

Serves 6

1¼ cups mascarpone cheese
½ cup confectioners' sugar
grated peel of 1 lemon
5 tbsp. milk
5 tbsp. rum
3½ ounces ladyfingers or
    champagne cookies
⅔ cup heavy cream
confectioners' sugar, to dust
for the meringues
2 egg whites
½ cup superfine sugar

1 Make the meringues: Heat the oven to 275°F. Place the egg whites and sugar in a clean, dry, greasefree bowl set over a pan of simmering water. Beat with an electric mixer until the meringue is very stiff and glossy.
2 Spoon the meringue into a pastry bag fitted with a large star tip. Pipe 25 small swirls of meringue on a nonstick baking sheet. Bake 50 minutes until firm but not colored. Increase the oven setting to 400°F and bake 5 minutes longer until golden.
3 Meanwhile, make the filling: Beat together the mascarpone cheese, sifted confectioners' sugar, lemon peel, and 2 tablespoons each of the milk and the rum. Cover and chill until needed.
4 Make the cake base: Mix together the remaining

milk and rum. Dip the sponge fingers into the liquid. Use them to line the bottom of a glass serving dish.
5 Remove the meringues from the oven. Reserve 15 for decoration and roughly crumble the remaining meringues. Fold these into the mascarpone mixture and add to the dish.
6 Whip the cream until soft peaks form. Spread this on top of the mascarpone layer. Decorate the trifle with the reserved meringues. Dust the top liberally with sifted confectioners' sugar before serving.

Fig and marsala trifles

This light Italian-style trifle is quick and easy to make. Mascarpone makes a hassle-free alternative to custard sauce.

Makes 4

7 ounces Madeira cake or pound
   cake, cut into bite-sized pieces
7 tbsp. Marsala or sweet sherry
8 amaretti cookies, crushed
¼ cup superfine sugar
10 fresh figs, quartered
2 tbsp. confectioners' sugar, plus
   extra for dusting
1 cup plus 2 tbsp. mascarpone cheese
a little milk (optional)

1 Put the cake pieces in a bowl. Pour 5
tablespoons Marsala or sherry over; set aside.
Divide two-thirds of the amaretti cookies between
4 tall glasses. Top with the cake; set aside.
2 In a pan, stir the sugar in ⅔ cup water until
dissolved. Bring to a boil. Lower the heat and
simmer the syrup 4 to 5 minutes. Set aside 8 of
the fig quarters; add the remainder to the pan.
Remove the pan from the heat and set aside to
cool.
3 When the figs and syrup are cool, divide
between the glasses. Beat the confectioners'
sugar into the mascarpone and stir in the
remaining Marsala. If the mixture is too stiff, stir
in a little milk. Spoon over the figs. Cover each
glass and chill 30 minutes.
4 Decorate with the remaining fig quarters and
amaretti cookies. Dust with sifted confectioners'
sugar before serving.

Raspberry syllabub trifle

This simplest variation on a classic makes a great standby.

Serves 6

3¹/₂ ounces ladyfingers or
  champagne cookies
3 ounces amaretti cookies
8 ounces fresh or frozen raspberries
1 cup fresh orange juice (about
  4 large oranges)
for the syllabub
²/₃ cup sweet sherry
2 tsp. grated orange peel
5 tbsp. superfine sugar
2 cups heavy cream
to decorate
3 to 4 ounces fresh or frozen raspberries

1 Break up the sponge fingers and place in a bowl with the amaretti cookies. Scatter the raspberries over and sprinkle with orange juice. Leave to soak at least 1 hour, preferably 2 or 3.
2 Make the syllabub: Mix together the sherry, orange peel, and sugar, stirring until the sugar dissolves. Using a wire whisk, gradually whisk in the cream, whisking until the cream just holds its shape.
3 Spoon the syllabub over the fruit and sponge in soft folds. Scatter the raspberries over. Chill until ready to serve.

Rhubarb and white chocolate trifle

This variation of an old-fashioned favorite of rhubarb and custard incorporates white chocolate for a new dimension.

1¹/₂ pounds rhubarb
1 tbsp. butter
4 to 8 tbsp. superfine sugar, to taste
2 tbsp. orange juice
3 tbsp. sweet wine, sherry, or brandy
for the cake
butter for greasing
2³/₄ ounces white chocolate
¹/₂ tsp. finely grated lemon peel
1 tsp. finely grated orange peel
¹/₃ cup all-purpose flour
³/₄ cup skinned toasted hazelnuts
3 eggs, separated
5 tbsp. superfine sugar
for the custard
³/₄ cup plus 2 tbsp. milk
³/₄ cup plus 2 tbsp. heavy cream
1 vanilla bean (optional)
6 egg yolks
¹/₄ cup superfine sugar
5 ounces white chocolate, roughly
  chopped
to decorate
²/₃ cup heavy cream
white and milk chocolate curls (see
  page 100)

1 Make the cake: Heat the oven to 350°F. Grease a shallow 10¹/₂ x 6¹/₂-inch pan and line it with nonstick baking paper. Roughly chop the white chocolate, then process in a food processor until it resembles bread crumbs. Transfer to a bowl and stir in the lemon and orange peels and flour. Process the hazelnuts in a food processor until ground, then stir into the chocolate mixture.
2 In a bowl set over a pan of simmering water, beat the egg yolks with half the sugar about 5 minutes until the beaters leave a trail when lifted. Off the heat, whisk 5 minutes longer until cool.
3 In a clean, dry bowl, beat the egg whites until stiff but not dry. Gradually beat in the remaining sugar to make a meringue. Stir the hazelnut mixture into the egg yolks and sugar. Stir in 3 tablespoons meringue to slacken the mixture, then, using a large metal spoon, fold in the remainder. Pour into the pan and smooth.
4 Bake 25 to 30 minutes until risen and golden brown. Turn out onto a wire rack to cool. Cut in half lengthwise, then into 1-inch-long fingers.
5 Make the rhubarb filling: Peel any tough rhubarb stalks and chop the rest into ¹/₂-inch pieces. Melt the butter in a large pan. Stir in the

rhubarb and cook over medium heat 3 minutes. Stir in the sugar and orange juice. Simmer 3 minutes longer, stirring occasionally, until the rhubarb is just tender and the juices are syrupy.
6 Drain the rhubarb in a colander over a bowl. Stir the wine, sherry, or brandy into the rhubarb syrup. Arrange the cake fingers in the bottom of a 2-quart glass dish and spoon the syrup over. Arrange the rhubarb on top.
7 Make the custard: Mix the milk and cream in a pan. Split the vanilla bean, if using, and scrape the seeds into the pan. Bring to a boil; set aside.
8 In a large bowl, beat the egg yolks with the sugar until pale and thick. Set the bowl over a pan of simmering water and beat in the hot milk mixture. Simmer about 20 minutes, stirring constantly, until it coats the back of a spoon; don't let the sauce boil or it will separate. Remove from the heat and stir in the white chocolate. Leave to cool completely.
9 Cover the custard with plastic wrap and chill 2 hours until almost set. Pour it over the rhubarb and chill until set.
10 Just before serving, decorate with lightly whipped cream and chocolate curls.

Master class: Making crème brûlée

Lemon crème brûlée with roasted peaches

Serves 4

sifted confectioners' sugar for the topping
for the custard sauce
3 egg yolks
finely grated peel of 2 lemons
2 tbsp. superfine sugar
1¼ cups heavy cream
for the roasted peaches
3 tbsp. butter
4 large peaches
2 to 3 tsp. light brown sugar
2 to 3 tbsp. brandy (optional)

1 Make the custard: Heat the oven to 350°F. Beat together the egg yolks, lemon peel, and sugar. In a pan, bring the cream to a boil. Pour the hot cream into the egg mixture, beating constantly.

2 Pour into 4 ramekins or a shallow baking dish, ½ to ¾ inch deep and 5 inches across. Set the dish(es) in a roasting pan and pour in enough hot water to come three-quarters of the way up the sides of the dish(es). Bake 20 to 30 minutes until the custard is just set. Leave to cool completely; cover and chill.

3 Roast the peaches: Heat the oven to 400°F. Heat 2 tablespoons of the butter in a shallow, ovenproof skillet. Add the peaches and simmer them in the pan, turning them until golden all over. Transfer the pan of peaches to the oven and roast 20 to 30 minutes until tender; baste the fruit several times with the butter as it roasts.

4 Heat the broiler to high. Evenly dust the chilled custard(s) with a generous amount of confectioners' sugar. Either broil, watching carefully, until the top caramelizes to a rich golden brown, or, if making individual brûlées, use a cataplana or a salamander as shown above (1-3). For a crisper topping, repeat this step once, or twice, again. If you have a blowtorch, use it to glaze the brûlée(s) for an even, controlled finish.

5 Carefully remove the peaches from the pan. Wipe the pan with paper towels. Melt the remaining butter in the pan, return the peaches to it, and sprinkle the brown sugar over. Roll the peaches in the sugar until they start to caramelize.

6 Sprinkle the brandy over—or, if you prefer, replace with water or orange juice—and let simmer to form a sauce.

7 To serve, place a roasted peach on each serving plate. Trickle a little of the sauce over and place a lemon crème brûlée to the side, or spoon some from the larger dish.

Orange cheesecake brûlée with orange sauce

With its brûlée topping, this easy cheesecake becomes an impressive dessert.

Serves 8

1 cup superfine sugar
thinly pared peel and juice of 2
   oranges
9 ounces Madeira cake or pound
   cake, cut into thin slices
4 tbsp. orange-flavored liqueur
1 cup plus 2 tbsp. quark cheese
1 cup plus 2 tbsp. mascarpone
   cheese
2 tsp. vanilla extract
1¼ cups heavy cream
scant 1 cup confectioners' sugar

1 In a heavy-bottomed pan over low heat, dissolve ¾ cup plus 2 tablespoons of the sugar in ⅔ cup water. Bring to a boil and boil without stirring 3 minutes until syrupy. Cut the orange peel into strips, add to the pan, and cook 1 minute.
2 Line the bottom of a 9-inch springform or deep, loose-bottomed cake pan with the cake slices, trimming so they fit in an even layer. Spoon 4 tablespoons of the orange syrup over.
3 Heat the remaining syrup until it makes a golden caramel; immediately immerse the bottom of the pan in cold water to prevent further cooking. Stir in the orange juice and liqueur, being careful because it may splatter. Return the pan to the heat, stirring until it becomes a smooth caramel; set aside to cool.
4 In a bowl, beat together the quark, mascarpone, remaining sugar, and vanilla. Whip the cream

until soft peaks form and fold it into the mixture. Spoon over the cake pieces and level the surface.
5 Heat the broiler to high. Dust the cheesecake with the sifted confectioners' sugar. Broil until just beginning to color. Leave to cool completely. Chill at least 2 hours or until firm.
6 Remove the cheesecake from the pan. Holding one end with an oven mitt, heat a long flat skewer over the burner until it starts to glow. Quickly and lightly scorch parallel lines across the cheesecake to caramelize the confectioners' sugar; reheat the skewer as necessary. Chill, then serve with the orange sauce.

Note:
The skewer will be irretrievably blackened so keep one especially for searing. This also makes an effective decoration on other sugar-dusted desserts.

The scorching principle used to such effect on the Orange Cheesecake Brûlée opposite can transform any flat-topped dessert dusted with confectioners' sugar.

Instant fruit brûlée

This is the cheat's way to brûlée—without any broiling or hot irons—and it works for most fruit mixtures.

Serves 6

6 passion fruit
2 large ripe mangoes, peeled, pitted,
   and cut into thin slices
5 ounces blueberries
1 cup plus 1 tbsp superfine sugar
2 cups heavy cream
2 tbsp. confectioners' sugar

1 Scoop the seeds from the passion fruit into a glass serving dish. Toss with the mangoes, blueberries, and 1 tablespoon of the sugar.
2 In a bowl, whip the cream with the confectioners' sugar until it just holds its shape. Spoon the cream over the fruit in the serving dish, piling it up in the center. Chill while you prepare the syrup.
3 In a small, heavy-bottomed pan, heat the remaining 1 cup sugar with 6 tablespoons water until the sugar dissolves. Bring to a boil and boil

until the syrup turns a midgolden-caramel color. Overcooked caramel is bitter; stop cooking the moment it turns this color—it also starts to smell marvelous at this point. Leave to stand 2 minutes, then drizzle the caramel slowly over the cream mountain so it runs down in little streams.
4 Serve immediately or leave at room temperature about 1 hour until the caramel starts to soften.

Light lemon and nutmeg brûlées

Inspired by the light brûlées of Spain, this cream-free version is deliciously scented—an extra surprise when you crunch through the topping.

Makes 4

2 lemons
2½ cups milk
1 cinnamon stick
freshly grated nutmeg
4 egg yolks
1 cup plus 1 tbsp. superfine sugar
2 tbsp. cornstarch

1 Pare strips of peel from the lemons and put them in a pan with the milk, cinnamon, and a sprinkling of grated nutmeg. Bring just to a boil. Lower the heat and simmer 10 minutes.
2 In a heatproof bowl, beat together the egg yolks and ¼ cup of the sugar until foamy. Stir in the cornstarch. Strain the milk over the egg mixture, stirring constantly. Return to the pan and simmer, stirring until thick and smooth. Simmer 5 minutes longer.
3 Pour the mixture into 4 shallow, flameproof dishes. Leave to cool and then chill at least 4 hours, or preferably overnight, until lightly set.
4 Heat the broiler to high. Sprinkle the dishes with the remaining sugar—you may need a little extra if the dishes are very shallow and wide. Place under the hot broiler or use a blowtorch to caramelize the tops. Serve at once, or chill until you are ready to serve.

Tiramisu cheesecake

Coffee, chocolate, and nuts give this cheesecake Italian style.

Serves 6

for the crumb crust
6 tbsp. butter, plus extra for the pan
1½ cups crushed ginger cookies
½ cup pecans, finely chopped
for the filling
6 ounces semisweet chocolate
⅔ cup heavy cream
1 cup mascarpone cheese
1 tbsp. cold strong black coffee
¼ cup superfine sugar
to decorate
1 ounce semisweet chocolate
1 cup mascarpone cheese
7 tbsp. thick plain yogurt
¼ cup pecans, roughly chopped
unsweetened cocoa powder for
 sprinkling

1 Make the crumb crust: Melt the butter in a pan. Stir in the crushed cookies and pecans. Press into the bottom of a lightly greased loose-bottomed 7-inch tart pan; chill.
2 Make the filling: Melt the chocolate in a heatproof bowl set over a pan of simmering water; leave to cool slightly. Whip the cream until stiff. Beat the mascarpone in a bowl with the coffee, sugar, and chocolate. Fold in the cream. Pour into the tart pan and smooth the top. Chill until firm.
3 Meanwhile, melt the chocolate for decoration in a bowl over a pan of simmering water; leave to cool.
4 Transfer the cheesecake to a serving plate. Mix together the mascarpone and yogurt and swirl over the top of the cheesecake. Drizzle the chocolate over and sprinkle liberally with the pecans and cocoa powder.

Chocolate-praline brûlées

Although looking and tasting sensational, these brûlées are deceptively easy to make.

Makes 6

²/₃ cup heavy cream
9 ounces good-quality semisweet
   chocolate, broken into pieces
4 tbsp. brandy
1 cup plus 2 tbsp. fromage blanc
½ cup plus 1 tbsp. superfine sugar
¼ cup slivered almonds, lightly
   toasted

1 In a pan, bring the cream just to a boil.
Remove from the heat and stir in the
chocolate, stirring frequently until the
chocolate melts and makes a smooth, glossy
sauce. Stir in the brandy, fromage blanc, and
2 tablespoons of the sugar. Pour the mixture
into 6 ramekins or dessert pots and scatter
the almonds over.
2 In a small, heavy-bottomed pan, heat the
remaining sugar with 3 tablespoons water
until the sugar dissolves. Bring to a boil and
boil rapidly about 5 minutes until the syrup
turns a pale caramel color. Immerse the
bottom of the pan in cold water to stop the
cooking; it will hiss.
3 Using a teaspoon, drizzle the syrup in a thin
stream over the almonds—don't drizzle over
too much or it will be thick and brittle. It will
set almost instantly, but, if left to stand, the
caramel slowly softens.

Peach and honeycomb fools

Turn peaches into an extra-delicious treat with the easiest of treatments.

Makes 4

1¾ cups fromage blanc
6 peaches, peeled and pitted
1 honeycomb candy bar, roughly
   crushed
sprigs of mint or balm for decoration

1 Put the fromage blanc into a bowl. Place the peaches in a food processor and process until smooth. Lightly fold the peach purée and most of the honeycomb into the fromage blanc.
2 Spoon the mixture into individual glasses. Decorate with the remaining honeycomb and sprigs of mint or balm. Serve immediately.

Almond palmiers with nectarine cream

Make the palmiers in advance; they'll keep in an airtight container for a week, or in the freezer for up to three months, but recrisp for a few minutes in a medium oven before using.

Serves 8

1 pound puff pastry dough, thawed if
   frozen
confectioners' sugar for dusting
1 pound store-bought white almond
   paste
¾ cup plus 2 tbsp. crème fraîche or
   sour cream
lime wedges, to serve
mint sprigs, to decorate
for the nectarine compote
12 ounces nectarines, skinned, pitted,
   and roughly chopped
4 tbsp. apple juice
¼ cup superfine sugar

1 Make the nectarine compote: Put the prepared nectarines in a pan and pour the apple juice and sugar over. Leave to stand 15 minutes. Place the pan over low heat and simmer until the nectarines are soft but do not collapse; leave to cool.
2 Heat the oven to 400°F. Line baking sheets with nonstick baking paper. On a lightly floured surface, roll out the dough to a 12 x 9½-inch rectangle; set aside. On a surface dusted with confectioners' sugar, roll out the almond paste to the same size. Lift the almond paste on top of the dough and press down lightly with a rolling pin.
3 Fold the long sides into the middle, leaving a small gap between them. Fold each piece in half to the middle again. Cut into 16 slices.
4 Place one palmier between two pieces of plastic wrap and roll out to a 4 x 2½-inch rectangle. Remove the plastic wrap. Repeat with the remaining palmiers and place them, well spaced, on the baking sheets. Bake 6 to 8 minutes until risen and crisp. Leave to cool on a wire rack.
5 Spoon the crème fraîche and nectarine compote over 8 of the palmiers. Top with the remaining palmiers and dust with sifted confectioners' sugar.
6 Serve with fresh lime wedges and decorated with sprigs of fresh mint.

Coconut cream with Malibu fruits

GIve a miscellany of summer fruit this totally tropical treatment.

Serves 8 to 10

2 ripe papayas, peeled, seeded, and sliced

1 pound strawberries, hulled and halved

8 ounces raspberries

8 ounces blueberries

4 tbsp. superfine sugar

4 tbsp. rum- or fruit-based liqueur

strawberry leaves or fresh mint for decoration

for the coconut cream

8 leaves gelatin

4 tbsp. rum- or fruit-based liqueur

2¼ cups vanilla-flavored fromage blanc

2½ cups coconut cream

½ cup superfine sugar

2½ cups whipping cream, lightly whipped

1 Make the coconut cream: Break the gelatin into a heatproof bowl and add 4 tablespoons water and the liqueur; set aside to soak 5 minutes. Place the bowl over a pan of simmering water, stirring occasionally until the gelatin dissolves.

2 In a separate bowl, beat together the fromage blanc, coconut cream, and sugar. Stir in the gelatin mixture. Fold in the cream. Pour into a large, glass serving bowl, cover with plastic wrap, and chill until ready to serve.

3 Place the fruits in a bowl, sprinkle the sugar over, and drizzle with the liqueur; set aside at room temperature.

4 Just before serving, pile the fruits over the coconut mixture and decorate with strawberry leaves or fresh mint.

Fast and Foolish

Spangled berry cream

Serves 4

Bring the juice of 1 orange and 2 tablespoons red-currant jelly to a boil in a small pan and boil rapidly for 2 to 3 minutes until thick. Stir in 12 ounces mixed berries, such as raspberries, strawberries, blueberries, and red currants; remove from heat. Using a slotted spoon, transfer 2 ounces of berries to a small bowl. Place the remainder in a serving dish and leave to cool a little. Whip $^2/_3$ cup whipping cream until soft peaks form. Fold in $^2/_3$ cup thick plain yogurt and grated peel from orange. Sprinkle 10 crushed amaretti cookies over berry mixture and swirl cream and yogurt on top. Spoon over reserved berries.

Meanwhile, place $^1/_4$ cup superfine sugar in a small pan with 1 tablespoon cold water. Heat slowly until sugar completely dissolves. Increase heat and boil rapidly, without stirring, until a light golden caramel. Remove from heat, let cool 1 minute, then quickly drizzle caramel strands on top of dessert. Chill until ready to serve.

Summer fruit sabayon

Serves 4

Place 2 beaten egg yolks and 2 ounces superfine sugar in a heatproof bowl and beat until well combined. Add grated peel of $^1/_2$ lemon and $^2/_3$ cup dry white wine. Set bowl over a pan of simmering water; do not allow bowl to touch water. Continue beating until sabayon is smooth and thick. Gradually stir in 4 tablespoons of light cream and beat for 1 minute until well combined. Arrange 1 pound mixed summer fruit, such as blueberries, raspberries, pitted cherries, grapes, and apricot wedges, in a shallow ovenproof dish. Pour the sabayon over and place under a hot grill until golden. Serve at once.

Quick apricot fool

Serves 4 to 6

Drain two 14-ounce cans of apricot halves in natural juice. Slice 2 of the apricot halves and set these aside. Purée the remaing apricots in a blender or food processor with 3 tablespoons clear honey and the grated peel and juice of 1 lime until smooth. Transfer to a mixing bowl. Gently fold in $1\frac{1}{2}$ cups ready-made custard and $\frac{2}{3}$ cup heavy cream, whipped. Serve decorated with the reserved apricot slices and some herb sprigs or pared lime peel cut into fine julienne strips.

Highland flummery

Serves 6

Melt 1 tablespoon butter in a skillet. Add 1 cup Scotch oats and stir-fry for 3 to 4 minutes until toasted. Add 1 tablespoon light Barbados sugar and remove from the heat. Whip $1\frac{1}{4}$ cups whipping cream until it just holds its shape. Gradually beat in 3 tablespoons of wildflower honey, 4 tablespoons Drambuie, and the juice of 1 small lime. Reserve 1 tablespoon of the oat mixture and halve the remainder. Divide the first half between 6 glasses and top with half the cream. Repeat. Sprinkle the reserved oat mixture on top. Decorate with raspberries and blueberries, grated lime peel, and mint leaves.

Currants in red-wine molds

Banish the childhood associations of gelatin-based desserts with this unusual treatment that suits the most grown-up of tables.

Makes 6

2 1/2 cups red wine
3/4 cup plus 2 tbsp. sugar
1 orange
1 1/2 pounds mixed red currants and
    black currants, or all red currants
2 envelopes unflavored powdered
    gelatin
6 fresh mint leaves

1 Pour the red wine and sugar into a saucepan Pare the peel from the orange, taking care not to include any pith. Squeeze the juice. Add the peel and the juice to the pan with 2/3 cup water. Bring to a boil. Lower the heat and simmer 15 minutes.
2 Strain into a pitcher, then return the juice to the pan. Add the currants and simmer 2 minutes. Strain again. Return the liquid to the pan and boil briefly. Remove from the heat and stir in the gelatin until dissolved.

3 Leave the syrup to cool, then chill until it is just starting to set; stir in the mixed currants. Rinse six 2/3-cup molds or ramekins with cold water. Place a mint leaf in the bottom of each mold. Spoon in the gelatin. Set the molds on a tray or plate and chill 3 hours, or overnight, until set.
4 Briefly dip the bottom of the molds in hot water, turn out onto small plates, and serve.

White chocolate and blueberry cheesecake

A toasted nut crust, creamy white chocolate filling, and a joyful fruit topping make this everyone's favorite.

Serves 8 to 10

for the crust
1 1/2 cups toasted hazelnuts
1/2 cup confectioners' sugar
1/2 stick butter, melted, plus more for
    the pan
for the filling
14 ounces white chocolate, broken
    into pieces
1 quart fromage blanc
1 1/2 envelopes unflavored powdered
    gelatin
for the gelatin topping
1 1/2 envelopes unflavored powdered
    gelatin
12 ounces blueberries
1/4 cup superfine sugar
juice of 1/2 lemon

1 Process the hazelnuts and confectioners' sugar in a food processor or blender until the nuts are finely chopped. Pour in the melted butter and process again. Press the mixture firmly on the bottom of a lightly buttered loose-bottomed 9-inch tart pan; chill.
2 Make the filling: Melt the chocolate in a heatproof bowl set over a pan of simmering water, stirring until smooth. Remove the bowl from the heat and beat in the fromage blanc.
3 Sprinkle the gelatin over 5 tablespoons warm water in a small bowl; stir until dissolved and translucent. Stir into the fromage blanc mixture. Pour over the hazelnut base; chill.
4 Meanwhile, make the topping: Sprinkle the gelatin over 4 tablespoons cold water in a small bowl; set aside to soak.
5 In a pan, heat half the blueberries, the sugar, lemon juice, and 1 1/4 cups water until the liquid is boiling and purple in color. Allow to cool slightly, stir in the soaked gelatin and remaining berries; remove from the heat and cool.
6 When the mixture is cool, spoon it over the top of the cheesecake. Return to the refrigerator about 3 hours until set.
7 To serve, carefully run a wet knife around the top of the cheesecake to loosen the gelatin before removing from the pan.

Winning the Toss

A bewitching battery of crêpes, pancakes, and waffles

Master class: Making crêpes

Basic crêpes

Makes 10 to 12

⅔ cup all-purpose flour
1 egg, plus 1 egg yolk
1¼ cups 2% milk
1 tbsp. sunflower oil, plus extra for frying

1 Sift the flour into a bowl (1). Make a well in the center, and add the egg, egg yolk, and half the milk (2).
2 Using a wooden spoon or a balloon whisk, beat the eggs and milk together, incorporating the flour at the same time (3). When the batter starts to thicken, gradually beat in the remaining milk (4) until the consistency is like light cream; make sure there are not any lumps. Beat in the oil. Cover and leave 30 minutes.
3 Heat the oven to 230°F (to keep the cooked crêpes warm). Heat a little oil in a heavy-bottomed 7-inch crêpe pan or skillet. Pour in enough batter (either from a measuring pitcher or using a ladle) to cover the bottom of the pan thinly (5), swirling the batter around the pan to form an even layer. Cook 1 minute, or until small holes start to appear on the surface.
4 Using a metal spatula, carefully turn the crêpe over (6) and cook 1 minute longer. Remove from the pan. Repeat this process until you have used all the batter. As you make the crêpes, stack them on a plate, separating them with waxed paper. Keep them warm, wrapped in foil in the low oven.

Notes:
* If the batter is left to stand, it produces better crêpes. However, you may need to stir in a little extra milk because the batter can thicken while standing.
* You can add a little sugar to the batter to sweeten it, or a good pinch of salt if you want to make crêpes with a savory filling.

Lace crêpes with raspberry and honey cream

Serves 6

2 eggs
⅔ cup all-purpose flour
pinch of salt
2 pinches of sugar
1¼ cups milk
1 tbsp. butter, melted
1¼ cups heavy cream
1 to 2 tsp. liquid honey, to taste
8 ounces fresh raspberries
vegetable oil, for frying
confectioners' sugar, for dusting

1 In a bowl, whisk together the eggs, flour, salt, and sugar until combined, then whisk in the milk until you have a smooth batter. Whisk in the melted butter, then pass the batter through a fine sieve.

2 Half-whip the cream and sweeten with the honey to taste. Fold in the raspberries and chill.

3 Heat a few drops of oil in a nonstick frying pan until hot. Pour the batter into a piping bag fitted with a very fine nozzle. Starting in the center of the pan, pipe a thin stream of batter and continue piping around, then across the pan to form a spider's web pattern with a diameter of about 5 inches. Cook until set, then turn over and cook for a few minutes more until brown and crisp; remove and leave to cool. Repeat with the remaining batter to make 12 crêpes; keep warm.

4 Place a crêpe on each plate, spoon some of the raspberry and honey cream in the center and top with another crêpe. Lightly dust with confectioners' sugar and serve immediately.

Lacy peach crêpes

Serves 4

3 peaches, halved and pitted
¼ cup confectioners' sugar
2 tbsp. crème de cassis
2 tbsp. fresh orange juice
⅓ cup all-purpose flour
1 egg
⅔ cup milk
oil, for frying
confectioners' sugar, for dusting
whipped cream or ice cream, to serve

1 Slice each peach into eight segments. Mix with the confectioners' sugar, liqueur, and orange juice; leave to macerate while you make the crêpes.
2 Sift the flour into a bowl, make a well in the center, and add the egg. Gradually beat in the milk to make a smooth batter with the consistency of light cream.
3 Heat 1 teaspoon of oil in a 7-inch nonstick skillet. Using a large spoon, drizzle about 2 tablespoons batter over the skillet's bottom in a lacy effect; do not tilt the pan or the batter will run together. Cook 2 minutes, then flip over and

cook the other side 1 to 2 minutes until golden.
4 Repeat with the remaining batter to make 8 crêpes. Fill the crêpes with the peach mixture and fold them in half. Dust with confectioners' sugar and serve with whipped cream or ice cream.

Apple and cinnamon sugar crêpes

Serves 4

2 tbsp. sugar
¼ tsp. ground cinnamon
⅓ cup all-purpose flour
1 egg
⅔ cup milk
oil, for frying
2 red apples, sliced
1 cup golden raisins
confectioners' sugar, for dusting
crème fraîche, sour cream, or ice
   cream, to serve

1 In a bowl, mix together the sugar and cinnamon.
2 Sift the flour into a bowl, make a well in the center, and add the egg. Gradually beat in the milk to make a smooth batter with the consistency of light cream.
3 Heat 1 teaspoon oil in a 7-inch nonstick skillet. Using a large spoon, drizzle about 2 tablespoons batter over the skillet's bottom in a lacy effect; do not tilt the pan or the batter will run together. Cook 2 minutes, then flip over and cook the other side 1 to 2 minutes until golden.

4 Repeat with the remaining batter to make 8 crêpes.
5 Sprinkle each crêpe with the cinnamon sugar. Arrange the apple slices and golden raisins on top. Fold them in half, or into quarters. Dust with confectioners' sugar and serve with crème fraîche, sour cream, or ice cream.

Master class: Making crêpes Suzettes

Crêpes Suzettes

The showiest restaurant dessert of all time, crêpes Suzettes are in vogue again. You can make them at home, with or without the theatricality.

Serves 4

for the crêpes
⅔ cup all-purpose flour
2 tbsp. superfine sugar
grated peel of 1 orange
1 egg
1¼ cups milk
2 tbsp. butter, melted, plus extra for frying

for the sauce
juice of 2 oranges
juice and grated peel of 1 lemon
3 tbsp. orange-flavored liqueur
5 tbsp. sugar
7 tbsp. butter
2 tbsp. brandy or rum

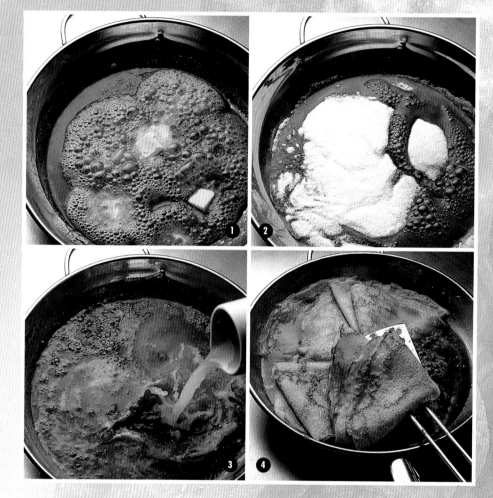

1 Make the crêpes: In a bowl, mix together the flour, sugar, and orange peel. Make a well in the center and drop in the egg, unbeaten. Start to beat the egg, adding half the milk in a steady stream and gradually pulling the flour into the egg mixture. Once all the flour has been incorporated, beat vigorously 2 to 3 minutes until the batter is smooth. Stir in the remaining milk and the melted butter to make a smooth, shiny batter that just coats the back of a wooden spoon.

2 In a nonstick 8-inch crêpe pan or skillet, melt a little butter. Ladle in a little batter, swirling the pan to coat the bottom as thinly as you can.

3 When the batter turns dark yellow and feels firm, using a metal spatula, lift up the edges and slide the spatula under the crêpe. Flip and cook 1 to 2 minutes longer. Transfer to a plate, cover with foil to keep warm, and make the remaining crêpes—this quantity of batter should make 8 crêpes.

4 Make the sauce: In a bowl, mix together the orange and lemon juices, the lemon peel, and the orange liqueur. In a heavy-bottomed skillet, heat the sugar and 1 tablespoon of the citrus mixture, tilting the pan occasionally, until the sugar melts and turns a toffee color.

5 Cut the butter into small cubes and add to the pan (1). Swirl it into the pan until it melts into the sauce (2). Pour the remaining citrus mixture into the pan (3) and stir until the caramel is dissolved and you have a glossy sauce.

6 Fold each crêpe into quarters and slide them into the pan (4), basting each one with caramel as it is added. Heat through for about 1 minute. When the juices are bubbling, quickly pour in the brandy or rum and ignite. Serve immediately.

Notes:
* Dissolving sugar is a tricky business. Be patient and don't be tempted to stir in the sugar because it can crystallize if you fiddle with it. Use a heavy-bottomed pan, preferably one that distributes the heat evenly. The sugar will start to dissolve in one place, so when this happens, tilt the pan to spread the caramel onto the undissolved sugar. Don't worry if the caramel forms lumps when the citrus mixture is added; when it bubbles up it will dissolve into the sauce.
* The crêpes can be made any time on the day you are going to serve them because they reheat well in the sauce, which can also be made any time on the day. Do not, however, put the crêpes into the sauce until just before serving or they will become gray and limp.

Breakfast pancakes

These are thick, almost juicy, and traditional maple syrup adds a spicy sweetness.

Makes 16

1½ cups self-rising flour
1 tsp. baking powder
2 tbsp. sugar
pinch of salt
2 eggs
1¼ cups milk, or equal parts
  milk and water
1 tbsp. butter, melted
olive oil, for frying
more butter and maple syrup, to serve

1 Mix together all the dry ingredients. Beat the eggs with the milk, add the melted butter, and pour over the dry ingredients, beating well.
2 Leave the batter to stand 5 minutes while you heat a big pan, preferably a 12-inch skillet. Lightly grease the pan with oil each time before using it. Stir the batter before making each pancake. Using a ladle, pour about 2 tablespoons batter into a quarter of the pan and wait until it settles before adding more (3 or 4 at a time is ideal—each one should be about 4 inches wide).

3 The pancakes will bubble up, becoming about ½ inch thick. When they are browned on one side about 1½ minutes, flip them over with a pancake turner and press down lightly. Cook 1 minute longer. Serve with a pat of butter and maple syrup.

Variation:
Although thought of as breakfast fare, these pancakes also suit ice cream or fruit purées for dessert. Or flavor the batter with 1 scant teaspoon of cinnamon.

Breakfast Pancakes opposite, dripping with maple syrup, can make a buffet table dessert to accompany fruit or fruit compotes.

Lemon crêpes

Serves 4

⅔ cup all-purpose flour
pinch of salt
1 egg, beaten
1¼ cups milk
vegetable oil, for frying
4 tbsp. butter
2 tbsp. sugar
pared peel and juice of 1 orange
7 tbsp. lemon curd
2 tbsp. brandy (optional)

1 Sift the flour and salt into a bowl, add the egg, and beat well. Gradually beat in the milk to make a smooth batter.
2 Heat a little of the oil in a skillet and pour in enough batter to coat the bottom of the pan thinly. Cook 1 to 2 minutes, turn over, and cook until golden; transfer to a plate. Repeat with the remaining batter to make 8 crêpes.
3 Melt the butter in the pan. Remove from the heat and stir in sugar and orange peel and juice; heat until the sugar dissolves.

4 Spread the lemon curd on the crêpes. Fold each crêpe in half and then in half again to form a fan shape.
5 Place the crêpes in the pan in overlapping rows and heat 1 to 2 minutes. Warm the brandy, if using; pour it over the crêpes and carefully ignite. Shake and serve.

Variation:
Use a good-quality marmalade instead of the lemon curd and replace the orange with a lemon.

Waffles with date and orange compote

Serves 4

½ cup port wine
½ cup sugar
finely pared peel and juice of 2 limes
2 oranges, segmented
4 ounces fresh dates, halved and
    pitted
½ cup shelled pecans
4 cooked waffles, warmed
confectioners' sugar, for dusting

1 Place the port wine, sugar, and lime peel and juice in a pan. Bring to a boil. Lower the heat and simmer 5 minutes, stirring occasionally, until the mixture is syrupy.
2 Stir in the oranges and dates and warm through 2 to 3 minutes. Stir in the pecans.
3 Dust the warmed waffles with sifted confectioners' sugar and serve with the compote.

Variations:
Replace the pecans with toasted whole or slivered almonds.

Buttermilk pancakes with apple, pecan, and maple syrup

Serves 4

⅔ cup all-purpose flour
2 tsp. baking powder
½ tsp. baking soda
1 tbsp. sugar
½ tsp. salt
2 eggs, separated
1 cup buttermilk
2 tbsp. butter, melted, plus extra for
    frying

**for the apple, pecan, and
maple syrup topping**
2 large all-purpose apples
2 tbsp. butter
¾ cup maple syrup
¾ to 1 cup shelled pecans

1 Sift the flour, baking powder, baking soda, sugar, and salt into a bowl. Mix together the egg yolks, buttermilk, and melted butter. Beat the liquids into the flour mixture until the batter is thick and smooth; don't overbeat. Beat the egg whites until stiff. Fold them into the batter; set aside.
2 Prepare the topping: Peel, core, and quarter the apples; slice each apple quarter into 4 pieces. Melt the butter in a large skillet. Add the apple slices and fry until colored and soft. Meanwhile, in another pan, heat the maple syrup with the pecans 3 to 4 minutes until the syrup is thicker.
3 Make the pancakes: Heat a large nonstick skillet and brush lightly with melted butter. Drop 3 tablespoons batter into the pan. When bubbles appear on the surface, flip the pancake over and cook until browned. Transfer to a plate and keep warm. Continue until you make 8 pancakes.

4 Place 4 apple slices on each buttermilk pancake and top with a spoonful of the maple syrup. Top with a second pancake, 4 more apple slices, and a large spoonful of the maple syrup. Repeat with the remaining ingredients to make 3 more stacks of pancakes. Serve at once.

Variation:
For a blueberry and cinnamon topping, place 8 ounces fresh or frozen blueberries in a pan with ¼ cup light brown sugar and ¼ cup water. Simmer until the blueberries are soft—this takes about 2 minutes for fresh or 5 for frozen. Blend 2 teaspoons cornstarch with 1 tablespoon water to make a smooth paste. Stir into the blueberry sauce with 1 teaspoon ground cinnamon. Bring to a boil. Lower the heat and simmer until thick. Serve hot or cold with the buttermilk pancakes.

The Upper Crust

Crust

The ultimate temptation of tarts, pies, and pastries

Torta di mandorle e pere (Almond and pear tart)

Serves 10

for the pastry dough
1 1/2 cups all-purpose flour
5 tbsp. superfine sugar
pinch of salt
1 orange
10 tbsp. unsalted butter, at room
    temperature
1 tbsp. dark rum
3 tbsp. apricot conserve

for the filling
5 tbsp. butter
5 tbsp. superfine sugar
3/4 cup blanched almonds, finely
    ground
1 extra-large egg, beaten
1 tbsp. dark rum
4 ripe pears, peeled, halved, and
    pitted
3 to 4 tbsp. slivered almonds
beaten egg, for glazing
confectioners' sugar, for dusting
lightly whipped cream or crème
    fraîche, to serve

1 Make the pastry dough: Put the flour, sugar, and salt in a bowl. Using a zester or grater, remove the peel from the orange and add to the flour. Make a well in the center. Roughly break up the butter with your fingers and add it to the flour. Using a round-bladed knife, cut the butter into the flour, shaking the bowl so any larger pieces come to the surface. Keep cutting until all the butter is in tiny pieces; work the mixture with your hands to break it up even more. Add the rum and about 3 tablespoons cold water and work together to make a ball, adding a little more water if it feels dry. Wipe the dough around the bowl to collect the bits; it should be slightly damp, never dry. Wrap in plastic wrap and chill 15 minutes.

2 Cut off about one-fifth of the dough for the lattice top; wrap and return to the refrigerator. Press the rest into a flat, even ball. Put it in the center of a 1-inch-deep 9-inch tart pan with a removable bottom, and press evenly over the bottom of pan and work up the sides with your thumbs. If the dough feels thick at the sides, continue to press to thin it, letting the excess fall over the edge (trim off later). Cover with plastic wrap and chill 30 minutes. Meanwhile, heat the oven to 400°F.

3 Prick the dough case lightly with a fork, line with waxed paper, and fill with baking beans. Bake 12 to 15 minutes until the pastry no longer looks raw. Remove the paper and beans, and bake 10 to 12 minutes longer until pale golden. Spread the apricot conserve over the pastry shell while warm; leave to cool.

4 Make the filling: Beat the butter and sugar together until pale and creamy. Beat in the ground almonds, egg, and rum. Arrange the pears over the bottom of the cooled tart shell. Spoon the ground almond mixture over the top so you can still see some of the pears. Sprinkle the slivered almonds over.

5 Roll out the reserved dough and, using a fluted pastry wheel or sharp knife, cut into six 1/2-inch-wide strips. Weave the strips over the pears to make a wide lattice. Brush the strips with beaten egg. Return tart to the oven 25 to 30 minutes until the filling is set and the tart is golden. Dust with confectioners' sugar while still warm. Serve warm or cold with lightly whipped cream or crème fraîche.

(See the picture on page 64)

Crostata di fichi e limoni (Fig and lemon tart)

This tart is based on an ancient Italian recipe that involves boiling whole lemons, then slicing them thinly with their skins into the tart shell before topping with figs. This version is not quite so sharp, because it has a smooth and creamy lemon base, and the figs snuggle in an apricot and lemon glaze.

Serves 10

for the pastry dough
1 1/4 cups all-purpose flour
5 tbsp. superfine sugar
5 tbsp. unsalted butter, at room
    temperature
1 large egg
1 tsp. vanilla extract
salt

1 Make the pastry dough: Pile the flour on a countertop. Make a large well in the center and tip in the sugar. Roughly line the well with the sugar. Pinch the butter into pieces and arrange these around the sugar. Break the egg into the center and add the vanilla and a pinch of salt. Using a fork, break up the egg and start to bring in the dry ingredients, breaking up the butter. Gather all the ingredients together using only your fingertips. As you feel the butter breaking

down, rub it in lightly until the dough feels damper and there are not any lumps of butter left—just speckles. Form the dough into a ball, gathering up any dry bits around the edge. Knead the dough lightly until smooth. Wrap in plastic wrap and chill 15 minutes.

2 Make the filling: Put the egg and sugar in a heatproof bowl and beat until frothy. Beat in the flour and 1 tablespoon of the milk. Heat the remaining milk in a pan, then pour onto the egg

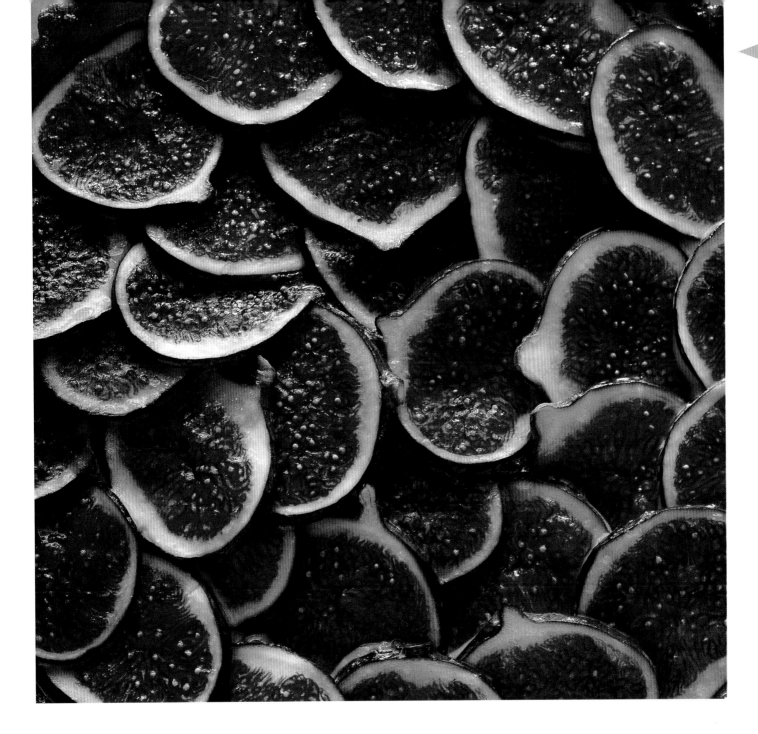

for the filling

1 egg

¼ cup superfine sugar

⅓ cup all-purpose flour

1¼ cups milk

2 tbsp. butter, diced

a few drops vanilla extract

grated peel and juice of 1 lemon

¾ cup plus 2 tbsp. crème fraîche or sour cream

5 ripe figs

4 tbsp. apricot conserve

lightly whipped cream, to serve

mixture, stirring. Return the mixture to the pan and cook over medium heat, stirring, until the custard is thick and smooth; do not boil! Remove from the heat and beat in the butter, vanilla, and lemon peel. Cover with waxed paper and leave to cool. When cool, beat in the crème fraîche.

3 Heat the oven to 400°F. Roll out the dough on a lightly floured surface and use to line a 1-inch-deep 9-inch tart pan with a removable bottom; lay the dough over the rolling pin and unroll it into the pan. Ease the dough into the edge of the pan with your knuckles. Trim the edge by running the

rolling pin over the pan. Prick the dough case with a fork. Line with waxed paper and fill with baking beans or dried beans. Bake 12 to 15 minutes, until the pastry no longer looks raw. Remove the paper and beans and bake 10 to 12 minutes longer until pale golden; leave to cool. Spoon in the filling and chill 1 hour until softly set; it should be just firm enough to slice.

4 Thinly slice each fig down from the stalk and arrange on top of the filling. In a small pan, melt the apricot conserve and lemon juice, and strain it. Brush this glaze over the figs and pastry edges. Serve the tart with lightly whipped cream.

Master class: Making cheesecake

Yorkshire curd tart

Serves 6

for the pastry dough
1 1/3 cups all-purpose flour
7 tbsp. butter, cut into small pieces,
    plus extra for greasing
2 tbsp. superfine sugar

for the filling
7 tbsp. superfine sugar
6 tbsp. butter, softened
2 1/4 cups cream cheese
grated peel and juice of 1 lemon
3 eggs, beaten
1/3 cup dried currants or seedless raisins
freshly grated nutmeg, for sprinkling
confectioners' sugar, for dusting

1 Make the pastry dough: Preheat the oven to 400°F. Grease a loose-bottomed 9-inch tart pan; set it on a baking sheet. Put the flour into a bowl and rub in the butter with your fingertips until the mixture has the consistency of fine bread crumbs (1). Stir in the sugar. Add 2 or 3 tablespoons cold water and mix to make a firm dough.

2 Knead the dough briefly on a floured surface. Roll it out into an 11-inch circle, using short, sharp strokes and giving the dough a quarter turn after each rolling. Flip the dough over the rolling pin, then lift it carefully onto the tart pan. Ease the dough into the bottom and side of the pan with your fingers, allowing it to flop over the top. Run the rolling pin over the top to trim the dough to a neat edge (3). Line the dough shell with waxed paper and fill with baking beans, dried beans, or rice. Bake 15 minutes. Remove the paper and beans and bake 5 minutes longer. Reduce the oven setting to 350°F.

3 Make the filling: In a bowl, beat together the sugar and butter 5 minutes until pale and light (2). Stir in the cheese and lemon peel, making sure the batter is well blended.

Gradually beat in the lemon juice, followed by the eggs, a little at a time.

4 Stir in the dried fruit. Pour the batter into the pastry case (4). Bake 30 to 35 minutes until the filling is set about 2 inches in from the edge and is pale golden on the surface; it

will set completely as it cools. Leave to cool in the pan 10 minutes on a wire rack. Transfer the tart to a flat serving plate. Sprinkle with nutmeg and a light dusting of confectioners' sugar. Serve warm or at room temperature.

Bitter chocolate tart with coffee-bean syrup

With its ultrasophisticated sauce flavored with dark-roast coffee beans, this is the perfect dinner-party dessert.

Serves 6 to 8

9 ounces prepared piecrust dough, thawed if frozen

whipped cream, to serve

for the coffee-bean syrup

1 1/4 cups sugar

1 ounce dark-roast coffee beans

for the filling

9 ounces good-quality bittersweet chocolate

5 ounces white chocolate, broken into pieces

7 tbsp. unsalted butter

1/2 cup superfine sugar

3 eggs, plus 4 extra yolks

1 Heat the oven to 400°F. Roll out the dough and use it to line a loose-bottomed 9-inch tart pan. Lightly prick the dough with a fork, then line with waxed paper and fill with baking beans. Bake 15 minutes. Remove the beans and paper. Bake 8 to 10 minutes longer, until the pastry is pale golden; set aside to cool.

2 Make the syrup: In a small pan, warm 1 cup plus 2 tablespoons water with the sugar over low heat, stirring occasionally, until the sugar dissolves. Add the coffee beans and bring to a boil. Lower the heat and simmer 4 minutes. Remove from the heat and discard all but 12 of the coffee beans. Leave these in the syrup; set aside to cool.

3 Make the filling: Break 5 ounces of the bittersweet chocolate into small pieces and place in a heatproof bowl with the white chocolate and the butter. Set the bowl over a pan of simmering water and stir occasionally until all the chocolate melts. Remove the bowl from the heat; set it aside.

4 In a clean bowl, beat together the sugar, eggs, and extra yolks about 10 minutes until thick. Grate the remaining bittersweet chocolate and sprinkle it over the pastry case. Pour the filling over. Bake 8 minutes until lightly set. Remove and leave to cool, then chill.

5 Serve the tart cut into wedges with a little coffee-bean syrup and some whipped cream.

Bitter Chocolate Tart with Coffee-Bean Syrup, opposite, served with a gobbet of cream, makes the most sophisticated and alluring of plates.

Pear crumble tart

Serves 6

2/3 cup all-purpose flour

2/3 cup whole wheat flour

1 tsp. baking powder

pinch of salt

1 tsp. apple pie spice

7 tbsp. butter, cut into small pieces

1/3 cup packed light Barbados sugar

2 large ripe pears, such as Comice

scant 1/2 cup crème fraîche or sour cream

1 egg, lightly beaten

2 tsp. sugar

1 Sift the flours, baking powder, salt, and apple pie spice together into a bowl. Add the butter and rub it in with your fingertips until the mixture has the consistency of fine bread crumbs. Transfer about one-quarter of the mixture to a separate bowl and stir the brown sugar into this to make the topping.

2 Heat the oven to 375°F. Add about 2 tablespoons cold water to the unsweetened crumble and mix to make a firm dough. Knead briefly on a lightly floured surface. Roll out and use to line a deep, loose-bottomed 8-inch tart pan or pie plate; chill at least 20 minutes.

3 Line the crumble shell with waxed paper and baking beans. Prebake 20 minutes; lower the oven setting to 350°F.

4 Peel and core the pears. Cut the flesh into small pieces and spread evenly over the tart case. Mix the crème fraîche, egg, and sugar together; spread over the pears. Sprinkle with the reserved crumble topping. Bake 45 to 50 minutes until the topping is crisp and golden. Serve warm or at room temperature.

Lemon and almond tart

Lemon tarts have enjoyed a considerable vogue over the last couple of years. This version is less aggressively lemony than some and has a delicious texture from the ground almonds.

Serves 6

8 ounces prepared piecrust dough, thawed
    if frozen
2 eggs
1¼ cups confectioners' sugar
4 lemons
7 tbsp. butter, melted
¾ cup blanched almonds, finely ground
confectioners' sugar, for dusting

1 Heat the oven to 425°F. Roll out the dough on a lightly floured surface and use to line a loose-bottomed 8-inch tart pan with waxed paper and baking beans. Bake 10 minutes. Remove the waxed paper and beans and bake 8 to 10 minutes longer until the pastry is crisp and golden. Lower the oven setting to 350°F.
2 In a bowl, beat the eggs and confectioners' sugar together until fluffy. Mix in the grated peel of 2 of the lemons, the butter, ground almonds, and the juice of all 4 lemons; don't worry if the mixture looks curdled—it won't affect the final result.
3 Pour the filling into the pastry case. Bake 25 minutes until the filling is set. Leave to cool on a wire rack. Serve dusted with sifted confectioners' sugar.

Pear and kumquat tart

Serves 8

for the shortbread crust

1½ cups all-purpose flour
⅔ cup butter, cubed
¼ cup superfine sugar
1 egg yolk

for the filling

2 pears
7 tbsp. unsalted butter,
   softened
½ cup superfine sugar
2 eggs, beaten
⅔ cup blanched almonds, finely
   ground
heaping 1 tbsp. all-purpose flour
8 kumquats
⅔ cup apricot jam or apple jelly
1 tsp. fresh lemon juice
thick plain yogurt, to serve

1 Lightly grease a loose-bottomed 10-inch tart pan. Make the crust: Place the flour in a bowl and rub in the butter with your fingertips until the mixture has the consistency of fine bread crumbs. Stir in the sugar. Make a well in the center and stir in the egg yolk to bind. Gather up the shortbread dough in your hand and press into a ball, wiping the bowl clean.

2 Roll out the shortbread dough between 2 sheets of waxed paper. Remove the waxed paper and line the tart pan with the shortbread, using your fingers to press it in and fill any gaps. Cover the shortbread with plastic wrap and chill for 30 minutes while you make the filling.

3 Heat the oven to 400°F. Make the filling: Core and quarter the pears; leave in a bowl of water. Meanwhile, using an electric mixer, cream the butter and sugar until light and fluffy. Beat in the eggs, followed by the almonds and flour. Spoon into the chilled base and spread evenly.

4 Drain and dry the pears. Make several thin parallel cuts across each quarter, taking care

not to cut right through. Using a metal spatula, lift each quarter and arrange on the filling, like the spokes of a wheel. Cut one of the kumquats in half and slice the rest. Place half a kumquat in the middle of the tart and cut the other into slices; arrange all the slices around the pears.

5 Bake 10 minutes. Lower the oven setting to

350°F and bake 20 to 25 minutes longer until golden brown.

6 Make the glaze: In a small pan, melt the jam with the lemon juice 1 to 2 minutes. Pass this glaze through a fine strainer into a bowl. Remove the tart from the oven and brush the glaze over it. Serve warm or at room temperature, with a dollop of yogurt.

Caramelized banana tarts with vanilla custard sauce

Bananas and custard are a marriage made in heaven. A cinnamon-sugar glaze makes it even more special.

Makes 4

½ cup all-purpose flour
2 tsp. confectioners' sugar
3 tbsp. margarine or butter
1 large egg yolk, lightly beaten
2 tbsp. sugar
½ tsp. ground cinnamon
1 recipe quantity of custard sauce
    (see page 40)
2 bananas, thinly sliced
juice of 1 lemon
a few drops of vanilla extract

1 Sift the flour and confectioners' sugar into a bowl. Rub in the margarine or butter until the mixture has the consistency of bread crumbs. Stir in the egg yolk and enough water to bind it without making a sticky dough. Divide the dough into 4 pieces. Roll out each piece to a thin 5-inch circle. Use to line 4 shallow loose-bottomed 4-inch tart pans. Prick with a fork and chill 20 minutes. Heat the oven to 375°F.
2 Bake the tart cases about 20 minutes until crisp and pale golden. Meanwhile, mix together the sugar and cinnamon.

3 Make the custard as described on page 40; keep it warm.
4 Heat the broiler to high. Put the tart cases on the broiler rack. Toss the bananas in the lemon juice. Arrange the banana slices in the pastry cases to cover. Sprinkle the cinnamon sugar thickly over the fruit. Broil 2 to 3 minutes until the tops are bubbling and golden.
5 Arrange the tarts on individual plates. Stir the vanilla extract into the custard and spoon this around them. Serve immediately.

Mixed berry pie

Serves 4

1 cup oatmeal
1½ cups shredded coconut
1 stick butter, softened
whipped cream, to serve
for the filling
3 tbsp. all-purpose flour
pinch of salt
¼ cup superfine sugar
3 egg yolks
1¼ cups milk
grated peel of 1 lemon
3 tbsp. heavy cream
12 ounces mixed soft berries, such as
    strawberries, raspberries, red
    currants, and blackberries

1 Heat the oven to 300°F. Mix together the oatmeal, coconut, and butter. Press firmly into the bottom and side of a loose-bottomed 8-inch tart pan. Bake 15 minutes; leave to cool completely.
2 Make the filling: Sift the flour and salt into a bowl. In another large bowl, beat the sugar and egg yolks together until thick and creamy. Gradually stir in the flour.
3 In a small pan, heat the milk and lemon peel. Bring to a simmer. Leave to cool slightly; pour into the flour mixture, stirring constantly. Tip into a small pan and bring to a boil. Cook, stirring constantly, until thick, about 2 minutes.
4 Leave to cool, stirring occasionally to prevent a skin from forming. Fold in the cream. Pour into the case. Pile the berries on top. Chill and serve with whipped cream.

Satsuma and raisin pie

Serves 4 to 6

8 ounces prepared piecrust dough,
    thawed if frozen
1¼ cups seedless raisins
2 tbsp. light brown sugar
4 satsumas
2 bananas, mashed
20 blanched almonds, finely ground
beaten egg or milk, to glaze
¾ cup thick plain yogurt, to serve

1 Heat the oven to 400°F. Set aside one-quarter of the dough. Roll out the rest on a floured board into a circle a little larger than an 8-inch pie plate. Use to line the pie plate and trim the edges.
2 Mix together the raisins and sugar. Peel and segment the satsumas over the raisin mixture to catch any juices. Cut the segments into pieces. Stir the satsuma pieces into the raisin mixture with the bananas and almonds. Spoon into the piecrust; level the surface.
3 Roll out the reserved dough into a 9-inch-long strip. Cut it lengthwise into narrow strips. Arrange the strips over the filling to form a lattice pattern, sticking down the ends with a little water. Brush with beaten egg or milk to glaze.
4 Bake about 25 minutes until just set. Serve either warm or at room temperature, cut into wedges and topped with a generous dollop of plain yogurt.

French apple tart

This wonderfully rich, tangy fruit tart comes from the Alsace region of France. The flavor of the apples is all-important and many of the fragrant varieties work very well. Depending on the time of year, try Baldwin, Rome Beauty, Winesap, or York.

Serves 6 to 8

for the pastry dough
1 cup plus 2½ tbsp. all-purpose flour
pinch of salt
6 tbsp. butter, chilled and cut into
    small pieces
2 tbsp. superfine sugar
1 egg yolk

for the filling
9 crisp all-purpose apples
juice of 1 lemon
¼ cup superfine sugar
pat of butter
½ cup apricot jam

1 Sift the flour and salt into a bowl or food processor. If making the pastry by hand, rub the butter into the flour until it has the consistency of fine bread crumbs. Stir in the sugar, egg yolk, and 2 tablespoons water and work into a dough. If using a processor, add the butter and sugar to the flour and salt; process 10 to 15 seconds. Add the egg yolk and 2 tablespoons water and process until a dough forms. Wrap in plastic wrap and chill 30 minutes.

2 Heat the oven to 400°F. Prepare the filling: Peel, core, and chop 6 of the apples; place them in a pan. Add half the lemon juice and 2 tablespoons water. Cover and cook over low heat 15 to 20 minutes, stirring occasionally, until the apples are tender. Stir in half the sugar and all the butter. Cook 2 to 3 minutes longer, stirring to a pulp; set aside.

3 Meanwhile, roll out the chilled dough and use to line a loose-bottomed 10-inch tart pan. Prick the bottom all over with a fork. Line the dough shell with waxed paper and fill with a layer of dried beans. Bake 10 minutes. Remove the paper and beans and bake 5 minutes longer.

4 Lower the oven setting to 350°F. Peel, quarter, core, and thinly slice the remaining 3 apples; toss the slices in the remaining lemon juice and sugar. Spread the applesauce over the pastry and arrange the apple slices on top; save the smaller apple slices for the inside circular layer of the tart because they are easier to arrange. Bake 30 minutes until golden.

5 Leave the tart to cool slightly on a wire rack. Carefully remove from the pan. Meanwhile, melt the jam with 1 tablespoon water in a small pan and boil 1 to 2 minutes until thick. Push the jam through a fine strainer into a bowl. Brush this glaze evenly over the tart. Serve warm or at room temperature.

Note:
A food processor makes light work of making pastry dough, but do not overprocess or the baked texture may be tough.

Oranges and lemons basket

Serves 4 to 6

for the pastry dough
1 cup plus 2½ tbsp. all-purpose flour
5 tbsp. butter, cut into small pieces
2 tbsp. superfine sugar

for the filling
3 oranges
2 lemons
1½ cups light cream
6 tbsp. superfine sugar
2 eggs, beaten

1 Make the pastry dough: Place the flour in a bowl. Add the butter and rub in until the consistency of fine bread crumbs. Stir in the sugar, add 2 tablespoons water, and mix to a firm dough. Wrap and chill 30 minutes.

2 Heat the oven to 400°F. Knead the dough and roll it out on a floured board. Use to line a loose-bottomed 7-inch tart pan. Trim the edge and twist a wide strip of foil around the edge of the pan to hold the decoration.

3 Roll out the trimmings and cut into long thin strips. Brush edge of tart with water. Twist 2 long strips of dough together and press around the edge. Twist 2 shorter pieces of dough together and place on one side to form a handle. Make 2 more handles and attach to the sides.

4 Line the dough shell with waxed paper and fill with dried beans. Bake 15 minutes. Remove the beans and paper and bake 5 minutes longer. Lower the oven setting to 350°F.

5 Make the filling: Grate the peel from 1 orange and 1 lemon. Place in a bowl with the cream, ¼ cup sugar, and the eggs. Beat together, then pour into the tart shell. Bake 25 to 30 minutes, until the filling is just set.

6 Squeeze the juice from 1 orange into a small pan with the remaining sugar and a few thinly sliced strips orange and lemon peels. Heat until the sugar dissolves, then boil 2 minutes until slightly syrupy.

7 Remove the rind and pith from the remaining oranges and lemons; slice thinly. Arrange over the tart and pour the syrup and peel over. Serve chilled.

Blueberry and cranberry tartlets

Makes 6

8 ounces prepared sweet piecrust
  dough, thawed if frozen
flour, for rolling

for the filling

1 cup plus 2 tbsp. ricotta cheese
1/4 cup superfine sugar
1 tsp. vanilla extract
2/3 cup heavy cream
1 tbsp. all-purpose flour, sifted
1 3/4 cups fresh or frozen cranberries
  and blueberries

for the topping

3 large egg yolks
3 tbsp. sugar
3 tbsp. kirsch (cherry brandy)

1 Heat the oven to 375°F. On a lightly floured surface, roll out the dough and use to line six loose-bottomed 4-inch tart pans. Prick the bottoms with a fork and line with waxed paper and baking beans. Bake 10 minutes. Remove the paper and beans; set aside to cool.

2 Thoroughly beat together all the filling ingredients, except the blueberries and cranberries, until smooth. Divide the mixture between the pastry cases. Top each with the blueberries and cranberries.

3 Place all the topping ingredients in a heatproof bowl over a pan of simmering water. Using an electric mixer, beat until the mixture becomes thick and creamy. Spoon a little of the mixture over each of the tartlets. Place on a baking sheet and bake 15 to 20 minutes until golden and lightly

set. Leave to cool for 5 minutes. Remove from the tartlet pans and serve.

Variation:

Make this with any mixture of berry fruit, flavoring with any fruit liqueur.

Cranberry and almond tart

This is a delicious tart to make from the Christmas baking leftovers.

Serves 6

8 ounces prepared piecrust dough,
    thawed if frozen
7 tbsp. butter, softened
½ cup superfine sugar
2 large eggs
½ tsp. orange-flower water (optional)
2 tbsp. all-purpose flour
¾ cup blanched almonds, finely
    ground
½ cup fresh bread crumbs
2½ cups frozen cranberries,
    thawed slowly in the refrigerator
2 tbsp. apricot jam or red-currant jelly
2 tbsp. whole blanched almonds,
    toasted and roughly chopped

1 Heat the oven to 375°F. Roll out the dough and use it to line a loose-bottomed 8-inch tart pan. Line with waxed paper and dried beans and chill 30 minutes. Bake 15 minutes. Remove the foil and beans; set aside the pastry case.
2 Beat together the butter and sugar until pale and fluffy. Gradually add the eggs and the orange-flower water, if using it. Fold in the flour, followed by the ground almonds.
3 Scatter the bread crumbs over the pastry case to soak up the fruit juices and prevent the pastry from becoming soggy. Spoon about three-quarters of the cranberries into the case in a single layer. Spread the almond mixture over.
4 Bake in the center of the oven 30 minutes, until the mixture springs back when lightly pressed.
5 In a small pan, heat the apricot jam or red-currant jelly with 1 tablespoon water until melted. Add the remaining cranberries and warm through until the berries burst. Spoon onto the tart and then scatter the almonds over. Leave to cool.

Variations:
* Replace the cranberries with frozen red currants or black currants, or raspberries.
* Scatter untoasted almonds over the topping before baking.
* Sift confectioners' sugar over to serve.

Sour cream and apple crumb pie

Serves 8

for the pastry dough
1⅔ cups all-purpose flour
pinch of salt
6 tbsp. butter
4 tbsp. shortening
4 to 5 tbsp. cold water
for the filling
1 lemon
1 tbsp. all-purpose flour
1 tbsp. sugar
⅔ cup sour cream

4 all-purpose apples
for the topping
⅓ cup packed light brown sugar
½ cup all-purpose flour
½ tsp. ground cinnamon
4 tbsp. butter, at room temperature, cut into pieces

1 Make pastry dough as for piecrust dough (see page 84), omitting the orange peel. Roll out on a lightly floured surface to fit a round 9-inch pie plate. Trim the edges; roll out trimmings and cut out leaf shapes and make dough berries. Arrange around top edge of pie, overlapping slightly and

securing with a little water. Chill 15 minutes.
2 Heat the oven to 450°F. Make the filling: Grate the peel from the lemon and squeeze 2 teaspoons of juice. In a large bowl, mix the lemon juice and peel, flour, sugar, and sour cream. Peel and core the apples; cut them into wedges. Stir the apple wedges into the bowl. Spoon into the piecrust.
3 Make the topping: Mix all the ingredients with your fingers until you make coarse crumbs. Press the mixture lightly together to form loose clumps; scatter over the pie. Bake 10 minutes. Lower the setting to 350°F and bake 30 to 35 minutes longer until the apples are tender. Serve warm.

Puff the magic pastry

Blue cheese, pear, and pecan puffs

Serves 4

Roll out 1 pound puff pastry dough until ¼ inch thick. Cut out four 5-inch circles and chill. Beat 1 egg yolk with 1 teaspoon water and brush over the circles; do not let it dribble over the sides. With the side of a fork, score ¾-inch lines around the edges and prick inner area. Chill.

Heat the oven to 425°F. Beat the egg white until soft peaks form. Stir in 3½ ounces crumbled blue cheese. Fold in 2½ tablespoons chopped pecans with 2 teaspoons heavy cream, and a pinch each thyme and pepper. Chill. Peel and core 4 pears, reserving the stalks. Cut each into 16 slices. Melt 2 tablespoons butter with ¼ teaspoon sugar in a large skillet. Fry half the slices until soft and lightly brown. Cook the rest in the same way; cool. In the center of each dough circle, pile one-quarter of the filling and arrange pear slices around it. Bake 15 minutes until golden. Stick a pear stalk in the middle of each and scatter with a little more thyme and pecans.

Tropical mango tart

Serves 4

Heat the oven to 400°F. Roll out 9 ounces puff pastry dough and cut out a 12 x 8-inch rectangle. Place on a greased baking sheet and prick with a fork. Spread 2 tablespoons lemon curd over the dough, leaving a 1-inch border. Arrange 18 ounces drained canned mango slices in syrup in overlapping rows to cover lemon curd, leaving a 1-inch border of dough. Using the back of a knife, make a small rim around the dough edge. Bake 20 to 25 minutes until the pastry is golden brown. Decorate the tart with coconut shavings.

Quick rhubarb tarts

Makes 2

Heat the oven to 400°F. Roll out 6 ounces puff pastry dough and cut out two 5-inch circles. Transfer to a greased baking sheet and prick all over with a fork. Bake 8 minutes until puffed and lightly golden. Meanwhile, put $1\frac{1}{2}$ cups chopped rhubarb, 1 tablespoon sugar, and 1 teaspoon ground ginger in a small pan with 2 tablespoons water. Simmer 4 minutes, or until the rhubarb is tender. Stir in 1 tablespoon finely ground blanched almonds. Spoon mixture on top of the pastry circle. Sprinkle 2 teaspoons brown sugar over. Bake 5 minutes longer until golden. Serve hot with sour cream or custard sauce.

Pear and walnut slices

Serves 4

Preheat the oven to 400°F. Roll $5\frac{1}{2}$ ounces puff pastry dough out to a thickness of about $\frac{1}{8}$ inch and cut it into four $3\frac{1}{2}$ x $4\frac{1}{2}$-inch rectangles. Place on a large baking sheet. Use a knife to score a $\frac{1}{2}$-inch border around the edges and mark with a crisscross pattern. Peel, halve, and core 2 firm but ripe pears. Then thinly slice the pears, not cutting all the way through at the top of each pear. Lift a halved pear onto each pastry rectangle and fan out the slices. Brush the pears with lemon juice and sprinkle with 2 tablespoons sugar. Bake 20 minutes until the pastry is golden and well risen. Remove from the oven, brush with 2 tablespoons maple syrup, and scatter 1 ounce walnut pieces over it. Serve warm with cream.

Tarte tatin

Serves 6

12 ounces puff pastry dough, thawed
   if frozen
6 to 8 firm, crisp all-purpose apples
juice of 2 lemons
10 tbsp. unsalted butter, at room
   temperature
3/4 to 1 cup superfine sugar, to taste
crème fraîche, to serve

1 Heat the oven to 425°F. Roll out the dough into a 12-inch circle about 1/8 inch thick; if it is any thicker, the pastry won't bake properly. Place on a board, cover, and chill at least 30 minutes.
2 Meanwhile, peel, core, and halve the apples. In a 10-inch heavy-bottomed, ovenproof skillet, using a metal spatula, spread two-thirds of the butter evenly all over the bottom of the pan. Sprinkle two thirds of the sugar over, distributing it evenly. Starting at the outside edge of the pan, arrange the apple halves, cut sides up, around the pan. After a full circle of halves is in place, fill the middle. Pack the apples closely together because they will shrink during baking. Sprinkle the apples with the remaining sugar and dot with the remaining butter.
3 Place the pan over medium-to-high heat and move it around slowly and carefully to distribute the heat evenly; do not let the mixture splash and make sure the butter and sugar do not burn or

blacken. Cook until golden and caramelized; this should take 20 to 30 minutes.
4 Allow to cool a little until steam stops rising. Lay the chilled dough circle on top of the apples. Tuck the edges down the side of the pan so, when it is inverted, the edge will hold in the apple, juices, and caramel. Bake 10 minutes until the puff pastry is puffed and golden. Reduce oven to 350°F and cook 10 to 15 minutes more until pastry is crisp.
5 Remove from the oven, leave to cool 5 minutes, then, using a metal spatula, carefully loosen around the edges of the tart. Place a plate or tray larger than the pan on top; quickly turn the pan upside down so the tart inverts onto the plate. Using the spatula, guide any apples that have become loose back into place; leave to cool.
6 Cut the tart into wedges and serve with crème fraîche.

Quick apricot and pine nut tatin

Using canned apricots lets you make a stunning and delicious tarte tatin from ingredients in your cupboard.

Serves 6

14 ounces puff pastry dough, thawed
   if frozen
4 tbsp. butter
1/4 cup soft brown sugar
2 pounds canned apricot halves in
   syrup, drained
2 tbsp. orange-flavored liqueur
   (optional)
1/2 cup pine nuts
ice cream or cream, to serve

1 Heat the oven to 400°F. Roll out the dough into a 12-inch circle about 1/8 inch thick. Cover and chill at least 30 minutes.
2 In a 10-inch heavy-bottomed, ovenproof skillet, spread the butter evenly all over the bottom of the pan. Sprinkle the sugar over evenly. Starting at the outside edge of the pan, arrange the apricot halves, cut sides up, around the pan. After a full circle of halves is in place, fill the middle. Pack them closely together. Sprinkle the liqueur over if you are using.
3 Place the pan over medium-to-high heat and move it around slowly and carefully to distribute the heat evenly; make sure the butter and sugar do not burn or blacken. Cook until it is golden and caramelized; this takes 10 to 12 minutes.

4 Lay the chilled dough circle on top of the apricots. Tuck the edges down the side of the pan so, when it is inverted, the edge will create a rim to hold in the fruit, juices, and caramel. Bake 12 to 15 minutes to bake the puff pastry.
5 Remove from the oven and, using a metal spatula, carefully loosen around the edges of the tart. Place a plate or tray larger than the pan on top; quickly turn the pan upside down so the tart inverts onto the plate. Leave to cool a little.
6 While the tart is cooling, toast the pine nuts in a dry skillet until golden.
7 Sprinkle the toasted nuts over the tart. Serve cut into wedges with ice cream or cream.

Pear and almond tatin

Serves 6

for the pastry dough
1 ⅓ cups all-purpose flour
7 tbsp. butter, cubed
1 egg yolk
¼ cup superfine sugar

for the topping
4 tbsp. butter
3 pounds pears, peeled, halved, and
  cored
2 tbsp. brandy (optional)
2 tbsp. honey
2 tbsp. dark Barbados sugar
3½ ounces store-bought almond
  paste, cubed
½ cup slivered almonds, toasted

1 Make the dough: Place the flour in a food
processor with the butter and blend until the
mixture has the consistency of fine
bread crumbs. (Alternatively, mix the butter
and flour in a bowl and rub together with your
fingertips to the bread crumb stage.) Add the
egg yolk and sugar. Mix to form a firm dough.
Chill 30 minutes.

2 Heat the oven to 400°F. Melt the butter in a
9- to 10-inch ovenproof skillet. Arrange the
pear halves, flat side down, in a circle around
the pan. Cook 4 to 5 minutes, until they begin
to soften. Turn over and continue cooking the
other side. Pour in the brandy, if using, and
cook until the liquid reduces. Stir in the honey
and sugar and cook 4 to 5 minutes until the
pears are caramelized and a syrupy sauce
forms. Remove the pan from heat.

3 Place a piece of almond paste between each
pear. Roll out the dough and lay on top of the
pears. Tuck the edges down the side of the
pan. Bake 20 minutes.

4 Invert onto a serving plate. Scatter with the
toasted almonds and serve.

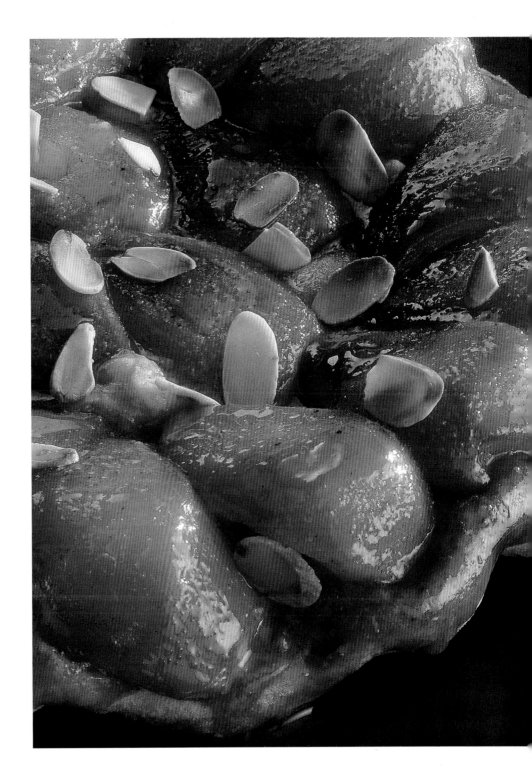

Treacle tart

Look for golden syrup, in its distinctive green and gold can, in gourmet delicatessens that import speciality ingredients from England.

Serves 10

for the pastry dough

1½ cups all-purpose flour
½ cup plus 2 tbsp. unsalted butter, diced
1 large egg yolk
1 tsp. sugar
1 to 2 tbsp. cold water

for the filling

2¼ cups golden syrup
2 cups fresh white bread crumbs
finely grated peel of 2 lemons
2 large eggs, beaten
⅔ cup oatmeal
ice cream or whipped cream, to serve

1 Make the dough: Place the flour in a food processor with the butter and blend until the mixture has the consistency of fine bread crumbs. (Alternatively, mix the butter and flour in a bowl and rub together with your fingertips to the bread crumb stage.) Add the egg yolk, sugar, and just enough cold water to form a firm dough. Cover and chill 30 minutes.

2 Heat the oven to 350°F. Roll out the dough and use to line a shallow 10-inch pie plate or quiche dish. Trim off the excess and flute the edges if desired.

3 Make the filling: Warm the golden syrup in a pan until thin but not hot. Remove from the heat and beat in the bread crumbs, lemon peel, eggs, and oatmeal. Pour into the piecrust.

4 Bake about 35 minutes until the filling is just set and turning to golden. Leave to cool slightly. Serve warm with ice cream or whipped cream.

Sweet potato pie with toffee pecans

Serves 8

for the piecrust dough

1⅓ cups all-purpose flour
pinch of salt
4 tbsp. butter
4 tbsp. vegetable shortening
grated peel of 1 orange

for the filling

1¼ pounds sweet potatoes
1 tsp. grated orange peel
⅓ cup packed light Barbados sugar
2 tsp. apple pie spice
2 eggs, beaten
2 cups light cream
3 tbsp. brandy

for the topping

2 tbsp. butter
⅓ cup packed light Barbados sugar
5 tbsp. light cream
½ cup pecans
confectioners' sugar, for dusting

1 Peel the sweet potatoes and cut them into chunks. In a pan of boiling water, cook them about 10 minutes until tender. Drain well. Press through a fine strainer; you should have about 1½ cups. Set aside to cool.

2 Heat the oven to 400°F. Make the piecrust dough: Put the flour and salt in a large mixing bowl. Cut the butter and shortening into pieces and rub into the flour with your fingertips to make fine crumbs. Make a well in the center and, using a knife, stir in the orange peel and 3 to 4 tablespoons cold water; don't stir too much or the pastry will be tough. Lightly press together into a ball. (You can do the rubbing and mixing in a food processor, adding only as much water as it takes to bind the mixture—stop immediately.)

3 Roll out the dough on a lightly floured surface until it is large enough to line a deep 9-inch pie plate or loose-bottomed tart pan. Trim the edge with scissors to leave a ½-inch overhang. Place a finger on the edge and push up the dough on each side with the thumb and forefinger of your hand to

make a wave. Line with waxed paper and baking beans or uncooked rice. Bake 10 minutes.

4 Make the filling: Mix together the sweet potato purée, the orange peel, sugar, and apple pie spice. Add the eggs and mix well. Stir in the cream and brandy. Pour into the pie case. Bake 40 minutes until the filling is just set; it should be a bit wobbly in the center. Leave to cool slightly.

5 Make the topping: In a small pan, heat the butter and sugar, stirring, until the sugar dissolves. Add the cream and simmer 2 to 3 minutes until the mixture bubbles and is slightly thickened. Remove from the heat, add the pecans, and toss. Spoon over the pie.

6 Dust the pie with confectioners' sugar to serve.

Glossy chocolate and peanut butter pie

Serves 10

for the crumb crust
14 graham crackers
6 tbsp. butter
2 tbsp. golden or light corn syrup
for the filling
1 cup cream cheese
2/3 cup chunky peanut butter
4 tbsp. sugar
1 1/4 cups whipping cream
for the topping
2 tbsp. sugar
2 tbsp. butter, in pieces
2 ounces semisweet chocolate, broken
    into pieces
chocolate curls (see page 100), to
    decorate

1 Heat the oven to 350°F. Make the piecrust: Seal the crackers in a large plastic bag and crush well with a rolling pin. In a pan, melt the butter with the syrup. Stir in the crumbs until evenly coated. Press into the bottom and up the side of a deep 9-inch pie plate or loose-bottomed tart pan. Bake 10 minutes; leave to cool completely.
2 Make the filling: In a bowl, beat the cream cheese, peanut butter, and sugar until blended. Reserve 1/2 cup cream for the topping. Whip the remaining cream into very soft peaks. Fold into the peanut butter mixture. Spoon the filling into the crumb crust.
3 Make the topping: In a pan, combine the sugar and reserved cream. Bring to a boil, stirring to

dissolve the sugar. Lower the heat immediately and simmer, without stirring, 5 to 6 minutes until very slightly thick and pale yellow. Remove from the heat and stir in the butter and chocolate until melted; leave to cool slightly.
4 Pour the topping over the pie and spread to cover completely and evenly. Chill, uncovered, about 1 hour until firm. Sprinkle with chocolate curls to decorate.

Note:
For a quick-and-easy way to make chocolate curls, run a vegetable peeler along the length of the flat side of a bar of chocolate at room temperature.

Amaretti and almond torte

Serves 6 (with second helpings)

1 1/4 cups heavy cream
3 large rosemary sprigs
9 ounces amaretti or macaroon cookies
1 stick unsalted butter, melted
2 1/4 cups mascarpone cheese
3 tbsp. superfine sugar
finely grated peel of 1 lemon, plus
    1 tbsp. juice
1 1/2 tsp. almond extract
3/4 cup plus 2 tbsp. thick plain yogurt
rosemary sprigs, roughly chopped,
    toasted almonds, pistachio halves,
    and confectioners' sugar, to
    decorate
Amaretto liqueur, to serve

1 In a small pan, bring the cream and rosemary sprigs to a boil. Remove from the heat; leave to cool.
2 In a food processor or blender, grind the cookies to fine crumbs. (Or put them in a plastic bag, seal, and crush with a rolling pin.) Reserve 5 tablespoons of the crumbs. Mix the rest with the butter and press into the base of a springform 9-inch cake pan; chill.
3 In a bowl, beat the mascarpone cheese with the sugar, lemon peel and juice, and almond extract until smooth and creamy. Remove the rosemary from the cream; discard. Add the cream, yogurt, and reserved cookie crumbs to the mascarpone mixture. Beat until soft peaks form. Spoon into the pan and swirl evenly over the bottom with a spoon. Chill overnight until firm.

4 To serve, cut into slices and place one slice in the middle of each plate. Decorate with rosemary sprigs and a few almonds and pistachios. Dust lightly with sifted confectioners' sugar and spoon some Amaretto over.

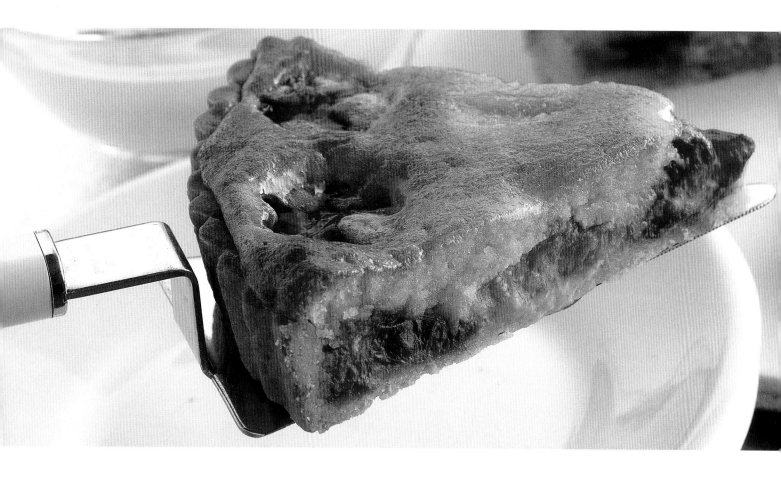

Plum, apricot, and almond tart

Serves 16

for the pastry dough
2⅔ cups all-purpose flour
pinch of salt
¾ cup plus 2 tbsp. unsalted butter, chilled
½ cup confectioners' sugar
2 large egg yolks

for the filling
1 cup plus 2 tbsp. unsalted butter, softened
1¼ cups superfine sugar
2 cups blanched almonds, finely ground
6 large eggs
8 plums, halved and pitted
8 apricots, halved and pitted

for the glaze
1 tbsp. apricot jam, warmed

1 Make the pastry dough: In a large bowl, sift the flour and salt together. Rub in the butter until the mixture has the consistency of fine bread crumbs. Stir in the confectioners' sugar. Add the egg yolks and mix well to form a smooth ball. Wrap in plastic wrap and refrigerate at least 20 minutes. Heat the oven to 400°F.

2 Lightly grease a loose-bottomed, fluted 12-inch tart pan and line the bottom with nonstick baking paper. Roll out the dough and use to line the pan. Prick the dough and cover with waxed paper and baking beans. Bake 20 minutes until golden. Remove from the oven and lower the setting to 350°F. Remove the paper and beans.

3 Meanwhile, prepare the filling: In a large bowl, cream together the butter and sugar until pale and fluffy. Add the ground almonds and mix well, then gradually beat in the eggs, one at a time. Arrange the plums and apricots, cut sides down, in the piecrust. Pour the almond mixture over. Bake 35 to 40 minutes until set.

4 Brush the tart with the apricot jam. Serve with crème fraîche or ice cream, if you like.

Smooth butterscotch tart

Serves 8

1 1/3 cups all-purpose flour
7 tbsp. butter
small can (7 ounces) of evaporated
   milk, chilled
1 1/4 cups packed light Barbados
   sugar
confectioners' sugar and unsweetened
   cocoa powder, for dusting
light cream, to serve

1 Heat the oven to 400°F. Tip the flour into a mixing bowl. Add the butter and cut it into the flour with a knife and fork. When the butter is in small pieces, rub it into the flour with your fingertips until the mixture looks like a pale yellow crumble. Shake the bowl to make any large lumps rise to the surface; rub these in too.

2 Using a round-bladed knife, stir 2 to 3 tablespoons cold water into the crumble until it starts to cling together. Pinch the dough together with your fingers, then wipe the ball of dough around the bowl to pick up stray crumbs.

3 On a lightly floured surface, knead the dough gently until it is as smooth as you can get it. Roll it out into a 10-inch circle, then flip it over the rolling pin and carefully roll it onto a loose-bottomed 8-inch tart pan. Press the dough into the side of the pan, leaving the excess to flop over the edge. Run the rolling pin over the top of the pan to trim off the excess.

4 Line the pan with waxed paper and fill with baking beans, uncooked pasta, or rice. Bake 20 minutes. Remove the paper and beans.

5 In a bowl, using an electric mixer, beat together the evaporated milk and sugar; after 5 minutes, the mixture should be thick and pale. Pour it into the pastry case and return to the oven 10 minutes. Leave the tart to cool in the pan, then slide it out onto a serving plate.

6 Cut into thin slices and dust with confectioners' sugar and cocoa powder. Serve with a drizzle of cream.

Note:
Make sure that you use authentic Barbados sugar, and not soft brown sugar, or the filling won't set properly.

Master class: Making cream-puff pastry

Paris-Brest

The Paris-Brest was created in 1891 by a baker whose shop was on the route of the annual bicycle race between Paris and Brest. The fancy gâteau's origins explain not only its name but the circular shape, designed to mirror bicycle wheels.

Serves 6 to 8

2 cups heavy cream
2 tbsp. confectioners' sugar, plus a little extra,
  to dredge
½ pound strawberries, halved
for the dough
1 cup all-purpose flour
7 tbsp. butter
4 eggs, beaten
2 tbsp. slivered almonds
for the praline
¾ cup unblanched almonds
scant ½ cup superfine sugar

1 Heat the oven to 425°F. Make the dough: Lightly grease a large baking sheet and line it with nonstick baking paper. Draw a 7-inch circle on the paper; set aside. Sift the flour onto a plate.
2 Melt the butter in a pan with 1¼ cups water. Bring to a boil; to prevent excess evaporation, do not let the water boil until the butter melts—then bring at once to a full rolling boil. Remove from the heat, tip in the flour and beat until the mixture is smooth and forms a ball, leaving the sides of the pan clean (1); do not overbeat—stop when the mixture is leaving the sides of the pan. Leave to cool slightly.
3 Beat in the eggs, a little at a time, until smooth and shiny with a soft, dropping consistency; the mixture should fall reluctantly from a spoon if given a sharp jerk. Spoon 10 mounds of cream-puff dough around the circle on the baking paper (2). Sprinkle almonds on top. Bake 40 minutes until golden. Split the pastry ring in half and return to the

oven 5 minutes; leave to cool on a rack. These puffs should be crisp on the outside and not doughy inside so they can hold a cream filling.
4 Make the praline: Place the almonds, sugar, and 1 tablespoon water in a pan. Heat slowly, stirring, until the sugar dissolves. Cook until the sugar caramelizes, turning occasionally. Pour onto an oiled baking sheet (3) and leave 15 minutes to harden (4).
5 Using a food processor, grind the praline to a coarse powder, or crush with a rolling pin. Whip

the cream with 2 tablespoons confectioners' sugar until stiff peaks form. Carefully fold the praline into the cream.
6 Spoon the cream mixture onto the bottom half of the pastry ring. Push in most of the strawberries, reserving a few for decoration. Replace the lid and decorate with the reserved strawberries. Dredge with confectioners' sugar and serve immediately.

White chocolate puffs filled with lemon cream

Serves 8

for the pastry dough
1 cup all-purpose flour
7 tbsp. butter
4 eggs, beaten
for the filling
4 egg yolks
5 tbsp. sugar
grated peel and juice of 2 lemons
4 tbsp. butter, softened
1 1/4 cups heavy cream
for the decoration
2 ounces white chocolate
confectioners' sugar, for dusting

1 Heat the oven to 400°F. Grease 2 baking sheets. Sift the flour onto a plate. Place the butter and 1 1/4 cups water in a pan. Bring slowly to a boil. When the liquid is boiling and the butter melts, remove from the heat and tip in the flour all at once. Beat quickly until a soft ball that comes away from the sides of the pan forms.
2 Leave to cool for about 5 minutes. Beat in the eggs, little by little, to form a soft, shiny dough. Dot heaped teaspoonfuls of the dough over the baking sheets, allowing plenty of space for them to spread. Bake 20 to 25 minutes until puffed and golden. Remove from the oven and slit from one side three-quarters of the way through. Return to the oven 5 minutes. Leave the puffs to cool on a wire rack.

3 Make the filling: Place the egg yolks, sugar, and lemon peel and juice in a small pan. Cook over low heat about 5 minutes, stirring, until the mixture thickens; do not let it boil because it will separate. (If this does happen, strain to remove lumps.) Remove from the heat and beat in the butter. Transfer to a bowl and cover tightly with plastic wrap. Leave to cool; chill.
4 Up to 2 hours before serving, whip the cream until stiff. Fold it into the lemon sauce. Spoon a little lemon cream into each cream puff and set on a tray or wire rack in one layer. Break the chocolate and melt in a bowl over a pan of hot, but not simmering, water. Drizzle the chocolate over the puffs. When set, dust lightly with confectioners' sugar. Transfer to a serving plate.

Profiteroles with chocolate sauce

Serves 4 to 6

1 recipe quantity of cream-puff dough (see page 90)
1 1/4 cups heavy cream, whipped, plus 2 tbsp.
7 ounces semisweet chocolate
2 tbsp. butter
2 tbsp. light corn syrup

1 Make the dough and bake the cream puffs as described on page 90. Using a pastry bag, pipe the whipped cream through the slit in the bottom of each cream puff. Pile on a serving plate.
2 Just before serving, melt the chocolate, butter, and syrup in a pan. Stir in the 2 tablespoons of cream and pour over the cream puffs.

Variations:
* You can flavor the cream for filling the profiteroles with coffee or vanilla extract, or a liqueur.
* Instead of the chocolate sauce, use simple caramel, a butterscotch sauce (page 137), mocha sauce (page 12), chocolate fudge sauce (page 111), or even a thick raspberry coulis.

Note:
Cream-puff dough can be made in advance and kept in the refrigerator for a day before baking. When it is baked, the puffs can be stored in an airtight container for 2 to 3 days, or frozen; recrisp in the oven.

Chocolate indulgence

Serves 6

1/3 cup plus 1 tbsp. all-purpose flour
4 tbsp. unsalted butter
2 eggs, lightly beaten

for the chocolate paste

3 1/2 ounces semisweet chocolate,
   broken into pieces
2 tbsp. dextrose or light corn syrup
confectioners' sugar, for rolling

for the coffee cream

2 cups heavy cream
5 tbsp. coffee-flavored liqueur
4 tsp. finely ground espresso or after-
   dinner coffee beans
6 ounces semisweet chocolate
unsweetened cocoa powder, for
   dusting

1 Heat the oven to 425°F. Lightly grease and dampen 2 baking sheets. Sift the flour. Melt the butter in a pan with 2/3 cup water. Bring to a boil and tip in the flour all at once. Beat with a wooden spoon until the dough is smooth and leaves the side of the pan.

2 Leave to cool for 2 minutes. Gradually beat in the eggs, a little at a time, to make a thick, glossy paste. Place 18 teaspoons of the mixture, slightly apart, on the baking sheets.

3 Bake about 20 minutes until well risen and golden. Make a slit in the side of each puff and bake 2 to 3 minutes longer until crisp; leave to cool.

4 Make the chocolate paste: Melt the chocolate and stir in the liquid dextrose or syrup. Beat until the mixture comes away from the sides of the bowl. Chill 30 to 60 minutes until firm.

5 Make the coffee cream: Lightly whip 2/3 cup of the cream with the coffee liqueur. Spoon or pipe into the puffs; set aside. Mix the coffee with 2 tablespoons hot water. Heat in a pan with the chocolate and remaining cream until the chocolate melts; leave to cool.

6 Whip the chocolate cream until thick. Use a little to secure 3 puffs together on a plate. Spoon the remaining cream over the puffs.

7 Cut the chocolate paste into 6. Roll out each piece as thinly as possible on a surface dusted with confectioners' sugar. "Polish" it by rubbing with the palm of your hand. Crumple to create folds and lay over the puffs. Dust with cocoa powder.

Brandy snaps with chocolate cream

Makes about 25

6 tbsp. unsalted butter
1/3 cup plus 1 1/2 tbsp. superfine sugar
3 tbsp. golden syrup (see page 84) or
    light corn syrup
1/3 cup plus 1/2 tbsp. all-purpose flour
1 tsp. ground ginger
finely grated peel of 1 lemon
2 tbsp. brandy
3 1/2 ounces semisweet or white
    chocolate, broken into pieces
3/4 cup mascarpone cheese

1 Heat the oven to 375°F. Line a baking sheet with nonstick baking paper. Melt the butter with the sugar and syrup. Remove from the heat. Sift in the flour and ginger. Add the lemon peel and brandy; stir together.
2 Place 4 heaped teaspoons of dough, spaced well apart, on the baking sheet. Bake 8 to 10 minutes.
3 Leave on the baking sheet about 30 seconds, then loosen one cookie with a metal spatula and roll around the handle of a large wooden spoon. Twist the spoon out. Repeat with the remaining cookies; leave to cool. If they become brittle before shaping, return them to the oven for a few seconds.
4 Melt the chocolate. Lightly beat the cheese and stir with the chocolate until smooth. Fill the brandy snaps using a pastry bag or small teaspoon.

Variation:
For dark and white chocolate fillings, use 2 ounces semisweet and 2 ounces white chocolate. Beat each type of chocolate with half the mascarpone cheese.

Mille-feuille of raspberries and Florentine cookies

Serves 2

2 1/2 tbsp. unsalted butter
3 1/3 tbsp. superfine sugar
1 1/2 tbsp. all-purpose flour
1/4 cup slivered almonds
1/2 cup mixed candied fruits, such
    as cherries, melon, orange,
    pineapple, and ginger, finely
    chopped
3/4 cup plus 2 tbsp. whipping cream
1 tsp. orange-flavored liqueur
1 ounce raspberries, plus extra to
    decorate
for the raspberry sauce
3 ounces raspberries
1/2 cup confectioners' sugar, plus extra
    for dusting

1 Heat the oven to 350°F. Line a baking sheet with nonstick baking paper. Lightly grease six 2 1/2-inch metal cooking rings, 2 1/2 inches deep, and place on a baking sheet.
2 Melt the butter in a pan with the superfine sugar. Stir in the flour, almonds, chopped fruit, and 2 tablespoons of the cream. Spoon the mixture into the cooking rings. Bake about 8 minutes, or until golden. Leave to cool on the baking sheet. Remove the rings and break up 2 of the cookies.
3 In a bowl, whip the remaining cream until soft peaks form. Fold in the broken cookies, liqueur, and berries.
4 Make the raspberry sauce: Blend the raspberries with the confectioners' sugar in a food processor. Push through a fine strainer to make a smooth sauce.
5 Place a cookie in the center of each serving plate. Place metal rings on top as guides and fill with the raspberry cream. Carefully remove the rings and place a second cookie on top of each. Spoon the sauce around. Lightly dust with confectioners' sugar and decorate with raspberries.

Mincemeat and apple strudel

Serves 6 to 8

1½ cups good-quality store-bought
   mincemeat
2 all-purpose apples, peeled, cored,
   and grated
6 ounces store-bought almond paste,
   chopped
6 sheets of phyllo pastry dough
2 tbsp. butter, melted
confectioners' sugar for dusting

1 Heat the oven to 400°F. Stir together the
mincemeat, grated apple, and almond paste.
Place 2 sheets of dough, slightly overlapping, on a
greased baking sheet. Brush with butter and place
2 more sheets on top. Brush with butter and
cover with remaining dough.
2 Spread the mincemeat along one long edge of
the dough to within 1 inch of the ends. Fold in the
ends and roll up the dough loosely. Brush with the
remaining butter and mark several times with a
sharp knife.

3 Bake 30 to 35 minutes until the pastry is
golden. Dust with confectioners' sugar and serve
warm.

Variation:
Macerate the mincemeat in a little brandy,
Calvados, or rum for 1 to 2 hours, or overnight,
before using.

Apple and pecan phyllo pie

Serves 4 to 6

10 sheets of phyllo pastry dough
4 tbsp. butter, melted
$1/2$ tsp. ground cinnamon
6 all-purpose apples
2 tbsp. lemon juice
$1/3$ cup superfine sugar
$1/2$ cup pecans
$1/2$ cup raisins or golden raisins
4 tbsp. apricot jam
sifted confectioners' sugar, for dusting

1 Heat the oven to 375°F. Trim the phyllo pastry dough to make squares. Place 1 sheet of dough in a greased loose-bottomed 8-inch tart pan. Combine the butter and cinnamon and brush over the dough. Place a second sheet of dough over the first one, but at a different angle. Continue layering the dough, at slightly different angles, brushing between each layer until all the dough is used.
2 Peel, core, and slice the apples; toss them in the lemon juice and sugar. Pile into the dough case. Bake 20 to 25 minutes until the pastry is golden and the apples are tender.

3 Sprinkle with pecans and raisins or golden raisins. Warm the jam and brush over the top. Dust with sifted confectioners' sugar and serve warm.

Variations:
* Plump the dried fruit in brandy overnight for an extra kick to the flavor.
* Grate some lemon peel and scatter a little over the butter between each layer of dough.
* Use walnuts or hazelnuts in place of the pecans.

Phyllo apple strudels

Any unused phyllo pastry dough can be stored in the refrigerator for two days, or in the freezer for one month.

Makes 8

8 sheets of phyllo pastry dough, each
    about 13 x 7 inches
7 tbsp. butter, melted
for the filling
$2 1/2$ cups peeled, cored, and roughly
    chopped cooking apples
juice of $1/2$ lemon
7 tbsp. light brown sugar
$1/2$ cup fresh whole wheat bread
    crumbs
$1/2$ cup golden raisins
1 tsp. ground cinnamon
for the topping
2 tbsp. sugar
confectioners' sugar, for dusting

1 Heat the oven to 400°F and lightly grease 2 baking sheets.
2 Prepare the filling: Stir together the apple, lemon juice, sugar, bread crumbs, golden raisins, and cinnamon in a bowl.
3 Unfold one sheet of dough and brush liberally with melted butter. Spoon on one-eighth of the apple filling to cover the middle third of one long side of the dough, leaving a small border. Bring the 2 short sides over the apple filling to cover it.
4 Roll the strudel over and over until all the dough is used up. Place on a baking sheet; repeat the process with the remaining dough and apple filling.

5 Brush the strudels with melted butter. Bake 15 to 20 minutes, or until golden brown and crisp.
6 Meanwhile, make the topping: Blend the sugar and 2 tablespoons water in a small pan. Heat slowly until all of the sugar dissolves. Spoon the syrup over the warm strudels. Dust with sifted confectioners' sugar to serve.

Surrender to Chocolate

A soft-centered assortment of chocolate desserts

Chocolate brownie cake

The creamy chocolate filling here turns the humble brownie into something very superior.

Serves 14 to 16

2 sticks unsalted butter, plus extra
    for greasing
1 pound semisweet chocolate
3 eggs
1 cup unpacked light Barbados
    sugar
1/2 cup self-rising flour
1 tsp. vanilla extract
1 1/4 cups pecans, roughly chopped

for the filling
2/3 cup heavy cream
3 1/2 ounces semisweet chocolate,
    broken into pieces

for the chocolate curls
3 1/2 ounces semisweet chocolate
3 1/2 ounces white chocolate

1 Heat the oven to 375°F. Grease 2 7-inch round cake pans and line their bottoms with waxed paper. Roughly chop one-quarter of the chocolate; set aside.
2 Break the remaining chocolate into pieces. Place with the butter in a bowl set over hot water and melt. Beat together the eggs and sugar. Stir in the melted chocolate. Sift in the flour and add the vanilla extract, the chopped nuts, and chopped chocolate.
3 Divide the batter between the cake pans. Bake about 30 minutes until the surface has a sugary crust and feels firm. Loosen the edges with a knife and turn upside-down on a wire rack covered with waxed paper. Leave the cakes in the pans until cool, then remove the pans.
4 Make the filling: Put the cream in a pan with the semisweet chocolate and heat slowly until the chocolate melts; leave to cool. Beat until stiff and use to sandwich the cakes together.
5 Make the chocolate curls: Melt the semisweet and white chocolate in separate bowls. Using a teaspoon, place thin lines of white chocolate on a marble slab or clean smooth baking sheet, leaving a gap of the same width between the lines. Fill the gaps with semisweet chocolate; leave to set. When just set but not brittle, push a sharp knife across the surface at an angle of about 45 degrees. (Alternatively, draw a potato peeler over the surface of the smooth side of a large chocolate bar to form curls.) Decorate the top of the cake with the curls.

(See picture on previous pages)

The Chocolate Brownies opposite can make the luscious dark heart of many desserts, topped with cloaking fruit and whipped cream or ice cream.

Chocolate brownies

Makes 9

3/4 cup butter, plus extra for the pan
3 1/2 ounces semisweet chocolate,
    broken into pieces
4 eggs
finely grated peel of 1 orange
1 cup packed light Barbados sugar
1/3 cup all-purpose flour
20 blanched almonds, finely ground
1/3 cup semisweet chocolate morsels
1/3 cup white chocolate morsels
confectioners' sugar and unsweetened
    cocoa powder, for dusting
ice cream or whipped cream, to
    serve

1 Heat the oven to 350°F. Grease an 8-inch square cake pan and line it with waxed paper. Melt the broken chocolate and butter together, stirring; leave to cool once they are combined.
2 Beat the eggs, orange peel, and sugar together until frothy, about 3 minutes. Stir in the cooled chocolate and butter mixture. Fold in the flour and the ground almonds, followed by the semisweet and white chocolate morsels.
3 Transfer to the prepared cake pan and smooth the top. Bake 30 minutes until well risen and just firm to the touch; leave the brownies to cool in the pan on a wire rack.
4 Cut into squares and dust with sifted confectioners' sugar and cocoa powder. Serve with ice cream or whipped cream.

Variations:
* For a classic brownie, omit the orange peel and juice and flavor the batter with 1 teaspoon good-quality vanilla extract.
* You can also add 1 cup chopped pecans or walnuts with the chocolate morsels. Or try seedless raisins, chopped dates, or chopped figs, if you don't like nuts.

Master Class: Making a roulade

Chocolate roulade

This is our version of the famous *bûche de Noël*, the popular French Christmas cake. It looks rich but, because it isn't made with flour, it is light in texture and more like a mousse than a cake. Don't worry if it cracks while you are rolling it up—this is a typical feature of a good roulade.

Serves 8 to 10

8 ounces semisweet chocolate
4 eggs, separated
½ cup superfine sugar, plus a little extra
   for sprinkling
butter, for greasing
for the filling
1¼ cups heavy cream
8 ounces canned natural chestnut purée
4 tbsp. confectioners' sugar, plus a little extra
   for dusting
1 to 2 tbsp. brandy (optional)

1 Heat the oven to 350°F. Line a 13 x 9-inch jelly-roll pan with waxed paper. Break 2 ounces of the chocolate into a heatproof bowl and set over a pan of hot, not boiling, water; stir until melted.
2 Pour the melted chocolate in a thin layer on a marble slab or cold upturned baking tray; leave to set. Holding a sharp knife at an angle of 45 degrees, shave off the chocolate to form curls. Place on waxed paper to set.
3 Melt the remaining chocolate as above. Beat the egg yolks with the sugar 5 minutes until pale and thick. Stir in the chocolate. Beat the egg whites until stiff. Fold into the chocolate mixture. Spread out in the prepared pan. Bake 15 to 20 minutes until risen and firm.
4 Sprinkle a piece of waxed paper with sugar. When the cake is baked, turn it out onto the paper; carefully peel off the lining paper. Cover the cake with a warm, damp dishtowel; leave to cool.
5 Make the filling: Whip the cream until soft peaks form; reserve 5 tablespoons of it for

decoration. Mix together the chestnut purée, confectioners' sugar, and brandy, if using. Using a large metal spoon, fold the whipped cream into the chestnut purée mixture.
6 Spread mixture over cake to within ½ inch

of the edges. From one short end, roll up, using the paper to help. Dust with sifted confectioners' sugar. Swirl the reserved cream in the middle and scatter the chocolate curls on top.

Notes:

* When melting chocolate, fill the pan with hot, not boiling, water and remove from the heat before placing the bowl for melting the chocolate on top. Make sure that the bowl doesn't touch the hot water.

* You'll know when the chocolate has set properly because it won't stick to your fingers when you touch it.

* Using a serrated knife, trim off any crisp edges from the roulade—you'll find it is much easier to roll up.

* The roulade will shrink, but that's quite normal.

* For best results, leave the roulade covered with the dishtowel until completely cool, preferably overnight.

* To slice the roulade cleanly, first dip a long serrated knife into hot water. Wipe the blade with paper towels after cutting each slice and dip again in water.

Alternative chocolate roulade fillings:

* Purée 1½ cups canned drained apricots by pushing them through a strainer. Fold into 1¼ cups whipped cream.

* Combine 1¼ cups whipped cream with 1½ cups frozen summer fruit. Serve when the fruit has completely thawed, which takes about 2 hours.

* For a dark chocolate flavor, fold 2 ounces melted semisweet chocolate and 2 teaspoons coffee extract into 1¼ cups whipped cream.

Torta al cioccolato (Chocolate tart)

The chocolate pastry for this tart doesn't need rolling—it is simply pressed into the tart pan.

Serves 12

for the pastry dough
2/3 cup all-purpose flour
1/4 cup unsweetened cocoa powder
5 tbsp. unsalted butter
10 blanched almonds, finely ground
1/4 cup superfine sugar
1 egg, beaten

for the filling
4 tbsp. butter
9 ounces bittersweet chocolate (look
   for one with 70% cocoa solids),
   broken into pieces
3 extra-large eggs, separated
1/4 cup superfine sugar
6 tbsp. heavy cream
1 tbsp. finely ground fresh coffee
confectioners' sugar, for dusting
heavy cream, crème fraîche, or sour
   cream, to serve

1 Make the dough: Put the flour, cocoa powder, butter, ground almonds, sugar, and egg in a food processor and process about 10 seconds until the dough forms a ball. Gather the dough together with your hands—the mixture should feel soft and slightly oily.
2 Press the dough into a flat even ball. Put in the middle of a loose-bottomed, fluted 9-inch tart pan, 1 inch deep. Press the dough evenly over the bottom and up the side of with your fingers. If the dough feels thick around the side, press with your thumbs to thin it out, letting the excess go over the edge (this can be trimmed off later). Cover with plastic wrap and chill 30 minutes.
3 Heat the oven to 400°F. Trim the dough by running the rolling pin over the top. Prick the bottom lightly with a fork. Line it with waxed paper and fill with baking beans or dried beans. Bake 12 to 15 minutes until the pastry no longer looks raw. Remove the paper and beans. Bake 10 to 12 minutes longer until the pastry feels firm;

leave to cool on a wire rack.
4 Make the filling: Melt the butter and chocolate in a heatproof bowl set over a pan of simmering water; leave to cool slightly. Meanwhile, beat the egg whites until soft peaks form. Don't worry if the egg whites separate a little while they stand. Beat the yolks and sugar until just combined and slightly frothy. Stir in the cream and coffee. Pour in the cooled chocolate. Using a large metal spoon, fold it into the coffee mixture together with the egg whites. The mixture should be light and mousselike in texture.
5 Spoon the mixture into the pastry crust. For a smooth, shiny finish, heat a large metal spatula under very hot running water. Shake off the water, then run the flat surface of the blade over the tart. Bake 20 minutes until the tart is firm around the edge and just set in the center; leave to cool on a wire rack.
6 Serve cool with a dusting of sifted confectioners' sugar and cream, crème fraîche, or sour cream.

Mocha roulade

This feather-light chocolate roulade with a slight coffee crunch may be made a day ahead.

Serves 8

butter, for greasing
6 ounces semisweet chocolate, broken
   into pieces
5 large eggs, separated
3/4 cup plus 2 tbsp. sugar, plus extra
   for sprinkling
3 ounces chocolate coffee beans
1 1/4 cups heavy cream
confectioners' sugar, for dusting

for the sauce
1 1/4 cups heavy cream
1 tbsp. finely ground strong-roast
   coffee, such as espresso
2 ounces semisweet chocolate, broken
   into pieces
2 to 3 tbsp. coffee-flavored liqueur

1 Heat the oven to 350°F. Grease a 14 x 10-inch jelly-roll pan and line with waxed paper.
2 Melt the chocolate in a heatproof bowl set over a pan of simmering water. Beat the egg yolks and sugar until pale and lightly aerated. Using a balloon whisk, gradually whisk in the melted chocolate.
3 Beat the egg whites until soft peaks form. Using a large metal spoon, fold one-quarter of the whites into the chocolate mixture to loosen. Gently fold in the rest, taking care not to knock out too much air. Pour into the pan and spread into the corners.
4 Bake 15 to 20 minutes until risen and just firm.
5 Sprinkle sugar over a large sheet of waxed paper. Invert the cake onto it; leave to cool.
6 Reserving a few chocolate coffee beans,

coarsely chop the rest. Whip the cream until it just holds its shape. Stir in the chopped beans.
7 Peel the lining paper off the cake. Spread the cream to within 1/2 inch from the edge. Starting from a short end, roll it up and slide onto a plate, with the seam on the underside. Dust with sifted confectioners' sugar; keep in a cool place.
8 Make the sauce: Slowly heat half the cream and the coffee in a pan until almost boiling. Remove from the heat and stir in the chocolate until it melts. Stir in the remaining cream and the liqueur. Pour into a serving pitcher.
9 Decorate the roulade with the reserved beans. Serve with the sauce.

White chocolate cheesecake

This cheesecake is dense and creamy, with the subtle taste of soft cheese and white chocolate. It is stunning served just as it is, but it is also wonderful decorated with strawberries and chocolate curls.

Serves 8

for the crumb crust
7 ounces chocolate graham crackers
4 tbsp. unsalted butter

for the filling
10 ounces good-quality white
   chocolate, broken into pieces
1¾ cups cream cheese
⅔ cup sour cream
2 eggs
1 tsp. vanilla extract

for the topping
8 fresh whole strawberries
chocolate curls (see page 100), to
   decorate (optional)

1 Heat the oven to 325°F. Make the crumb crust: Put the crackers in a plastic bag and crush using a rolling pin. In a small nonstick pan, melt the butter. Stir in the cracker crumbs and mix well. Using the back of a metal spoon, press the mixture evenly into the bottom of a deep 7-inch springform pan; chill.

2 Make the filling: Melt the chocolate (see page 103). In a bowl, stir the cheese, sour cream, eggs, and vanilla extract together lightly; do not overbeat because too much air makes the cheesecake rise, then sink, or rise, then crack. Stir in the melted chocolate until smooth; the filling will thicken slightly.

3 Spread the filling evenly over the crumb crust and smooth the top. Bake 50 minutes until the cheesecake feels firm around the edge and is slightly soft but set in the middle. It is important not to overcook the cheesecake, or it will become grainy around the edge.

4 Remove from the oven and leave to cool on a wire rack. Carefully lift out of the cake pan; chill. When ready to serve, decorate with strawberries around the top and, if you are using them, arrange some chocolate curls in the center.

Moist chocolate-banana loaf

This speedy "melt, mash, and mix" recipe bakes into a rich, sticky, and delicious cake. Sliced thickly and served with ice cream, it makes an immensely satisfying, easy dessert.

Makes a 9 x 5-inch loaf

½ cup plus 2 tbsp. butter, at room
   temperature, plus extra for greasing
1 cup packed light Barbados sugar
5 ounces good-quality semisweet
   chocolate
2 bananas, mashed
3 eggs, beaten
1⅓ cups all-purpose flour
2 tsp. baking powder
strawberry ice cream, to serve

for the frosting
3½ ounces good-quality semisweet
   chocolate, broken into pieces
2 tbsp. butter
½ cup confectioners' sugar
1 tbsp. milk

1 Heat the oven to 300°F. Grease a 9 x 5-inch bread pan and line it with waxed paper.

2 In a nonstick pan, slowly heat the butter, sugar, and chocolate until the chocolate melts. Stir and remove from the heat. Add the mashed banana and the eggs, then sift in the flour and baking powder. Stir to make a smooth, thick batter.

3 Pour the batter into the prepared bread pan. Bake 1 hour until the cake has risen and feels firm in the center when lightly pressed with your fingertips. Remove from the oven. Leave to cool in the pan on a wire rack 5 minutes; turn out onto the rack to cool completely.

4 Make the frosting: In a small, nonstick pan, melt the chocolate with the butter. Sift in the confectioners' sugar. Stir in the milk and beat well. Spread over the top of the cake only; using a flat-bladed knife, make swirls in the chocolate.

Leave to set.

5 Serve cut into thick slices, with large scoops of strawberry ice cream.

Variations:
* Add 2 tbsp. chopped candied ginger, chopped dried apricots, or chopped pecans or walnuts to the batter.
* Flavor the frosting with a little orange-flavored liqueur instead of the milk.

Chocolate puddings with white chocolate and Amaretto sauce

These are made in next to no time, yet taste rich and special. They should have a moist, slightly gooey center with a crisp crust, which contrasts excellently with the custard-style white chocolate sauce.

Makes 4

3½ ounces semisweet chocolate
7 tbsp. unsalted butter, plus extra for
  greasing
¾ cup superfine sugar
2 eggs, plus 2 extra yolks
⅓ cup all-purpose flour
for the sauce
3 ounces white chocolate
⅔ cup heavy cream
1 tbsp. Amaretto liqueur or brandy
unsweetened cocoa powder and mint
  sprigs, to decorate

1 Heat the oven to 375°F. In a pan set over a low heat, melt the semisweet chocolate and butter together until smooth; leave to cool slightly. Butter four ½-cup ramekins.
2 In a bowl, lightly beat together the sugar, eggs, and extra yolks. Beat in the melted chocolate. Sift in the flour and beat together.
3 Pour the batter into the ramekins. Bake 25 minutes until lightly risen and spongy to the touch. Turn off the heat but leave the puddings in the oven to keep warm.
4 Make the sauce: In a pan set over low heat, melt the white chocolate with the cream until smooth. Remove from the heat and stir in the liqueur or brandy.

5 Run a metal spatula around each pudding. Unmold, crust side up, into 4 shallow bowls. Spoon a little sauce around each. Lightly dust the bowl and sauce with cocoa powder and decorate with a mint sprig.

Variations:
* Add 2 ounces semisweet or white (or a mixture) chocolate morsels to the pudding batter for a contrast in texture.
* If you haven't got time to make the sauce, simply serve the puddings with good-quality ice cream and a splash of Amaretto or brandy.

White freezer cake with sticky brownie base

Keep one of these in the freezer at all times! The base is soft and sticky and the ice cream is simply the best.

Serves 12

for the brownie base

4 tbsp. unsalted butter, plus extra
   for greasing
5 tbsp. superfine sugar
scant 1/4 cup unpacked dark
   Barbados sugar
2 ounces good-quality semisweet
   chocolate
2 tsp. light corn syrup
3/4 cup walnut halves
1 egg
1/2 tsp. vanilla extract
3 tbsp. all-purpose flour
1/2 tsp. baking powder

for the ice cream

10 ounces good-quality white
   chocolate, broken into pieces
1 1/4 cups heavy cream
1 3/4 cups store-bought vanilla custard
   sauce

to decorate

2 ounces semisweet chocolate
unsweetened cocoa powder, for
   dusting

1 Heat the oven to 350°F. Lightly grease an 8-inch springform cake pan. In a small nonstick pan, slowly heat the butter, sugars, chocolate, and syrup, stirring until smooth and the chocolate melts. Stir in the walnuts; remove from the heat and leave to cool.
2 In a bowl, beat together the egg and vanilla. Stir into the cooled mixture. Sift in the flour and baking powder and stir together.
3 Pour into the prepared cake pan and smooth the surface. Bake 15 minutes until the outside

is crisp and beginning to shrink away from the side, but the center is soft; leave to cool.
4 Make the ice cream: Melt the white chocolate (see page 103). Whip the cream until just holding its shape. Beat in the chilled custard. Stir in the melted chocolate until the mixture is thick, smooth, and well blended. Pour over the cooled brownie base; tilt the

cake pan to level the top.
5 Melt the semisweet chocolate for decoration. Using a teaspoon, drop 12 neat blobs on the ice cream, at regular intervals, 1 1/4 inches in from the edge. Draw a toothpick through the middle of each blob, in the same direction, to make hearts. Freeze at least 4 hours until firm.
6 Serve dusted with cocoa powder.

Bitter chocolate puddings with chocolate fudge sauce

Makes 8

2 sticks butter, melted, plus extra for greasing
6 eggs
1¼ cups superfine sugar
1 cup all-purpose flour
½ cup unsweetened cocoa powder
9 ounces good-quality bitter chocolate, cut into ¼-inch cubes
softly whipped cream or ice cream, to serve

for the chocolate fudge sauce

1¼ cups heavy cream
¾ cup unsalted butter
⅓ cup packed light Barbados sugar
6 ounces good-quality bitter chocolate, broken into pieces

I Generously grease eight 3½-inch baking bowls or ramekins. In a large bowl, using an electric mixer, beat the eggs with the sugar until really thick, 10 to 15 minutes.

2 Sift the flour and cocoa together. Using a large metal spoon, fold into the beaten egg mixture, making sure you don't knock out all the air. Fold in the melted butter and chocolate cubes. Spoon the batter into the bowls or ramekins.

3 Cover the puddings tightly with foil, put them in a large roasting pan, and pour in enough boiling water to come halfway up the bowls. Bring to a simmer. Cover the pan and steam 45 minutes until the puddings are firm to the touch.

4 Meanwhile, make the sauce: Heat the cream, butter, and sugar in a small pan, stirring, until the butter melts. Add the chocolate and stir constantly until it melts; set aside, stirring occasionally to stop a skin forming.

5 When the puddings are baked, leave them to cool a little. Run a round-bladed knife around the edge of each and invert onto a serving plate. Serve with scoops of cream or ice cream and drizzle the sauce over attractively.

Variation:

* These puddings also cook well in the microwave. Use microwave-safe bowls and cover them with microwaveable plastic. Microwave 2 or 3 at a time on medium power 3 minutes; let stand 1 minute before serving.

* You can also make one large pudding in a 7½-cup heatproof bowl. After filling, make a pleated tuck in the middle of a double thickness of waxed paper. Put it over the bowl, tie firmly in place, and trim off excess paper. Cover with a layer of pleated foil, tucking the edge under the waxed paper. Steam for 1¾ hours.

(See the picture opposite)

Zuccotto

Serves 12

⅔ cup unblanched almonds
⅔ cup blanched hazelnuts
5 ounces semisweet chocolate, preferably with more than 55% cocoa solids
two 10½-ounce slabs of Madeira cake or pound cake
3 tbsp. brandy
5 tbsp. fresh orange juice
2 cups heavy cream
scant 1 cup confectioners' sugar
4 tbsp. apricot jam
confectioners' sugar, for dusting

1 Toast the nuts in a dry skillet. Roughly break up half the chocolate and melt in the microwave on high power 1 minute, or over a pan of simmering water (see page 103). Chop the remaining chocolate; set aside.

2 Line a 5-cup heatproof bowl with plastic wrap. Cut the cake into long, vertical slices ½ inch wide. Trim off the curved top from half of the slices, then cut these slices in half lengthwise on a slight diagonal to make wedge-shaped pieces. Trim each slice to the depth of the inside of the bowl. Arrange them, slightly overlapping, so they line the bowl.

3 Cut a slice of cake to fit the bottom of the bowl. Fill any gaps with small pieces of the cake. Stir the brandy and orange juice together. Spoon about two-thirds of this liquid over the cake in the bowl, making sure it is evenly soaked.

4 Whip the cream until stiff. Fold in the nuts, sifted confectioners' sugar, and chopped chocolate. Spoon half this mixture into the cake-lined bowl; spread evenly over the bottom and sides, leaving a cavity in the middle.

5 Fold the melted chocolate into the remaining cream mixture. Spoon this into the cavity and smooth the top. Cover the top with the remaining cake, cutting the slices to fit. Spoon the remaining orange juice mixture over.

6 Cover with plastic wrap and chill overnight, or for up to 2 days.

7 To serve, remove the plastic wrap and place a serving plate on top. Invert the bowl onto the plate; carefully remove the bowl and peel off the lining plastic wrap. Warm the jam; press through a fine strainer into a bowl. Brush the top and sides of the cake with the jam glaze. Lightly dust with sifted confectioners' sugar. Serve cut into wedges.

Chocolate Magic

Cappuccino cups

Makes 4

Pour ⅔ cup whipping cream into a pan. Sprinkle over 1 tablespoon unflavored powdered gelatin and leave to soften 5 minutes. Heat slowly until the cream begins to simmer and the gelatin melts, stirring constantly. Break 6 ounces semisweet chocolate into pieces. Place in a food processor with the cream mixture and process until the chocolate melts. Add a handful of ice cubes, 1¼ cups fromage blanc, ¼ cup sugar, and 1 tablespoon instant coffee powder. Process until smooth. Pour into cups; chill until set. Whip ⅔ cup whipping cream and pare curls from a small chunk of semisweet chocolate with a vegetable peeler. Swirl the cream on the "cups," dust with more coffee powder, and decorate with the curls.

Magic chocolate pudding

Serves 6

Heat the oven to 350°F. Grease six ⅔-cup ramekins with butter. Cream together 4 tbsp. softened butter and ½ cup packed dark Barbados sugar until lighter in color and texture. Beat in 2 large egg yolks. Sift together ¼ cup self-rising flour and 2 tablespoons unsweetened cocoa powder, and beat into the mixture. Gradually stir in 1½ cups chocolate milk until smooth.

In a clean bowl, beat the 2 egg whites and lightly fold into the chocolate mixture. Spoon into the prepared ramekins, place in a roasting pan, and fill the pan with water one-third of the way up the sides of the ramekins. Bake 30 minutes, or until the tops of the puddings spring back when lightly touched. The puddings separate to form a cake on top and a layer of chocolate custard beneath. Serve hot, dusted with confectioners' sugar.

Double-choc mud pie

Serves 6 to 8

Rub 7 tbsp. lightly salted butter into 1⅓ cups flour with a pinch of salt until it resembles bread crumbs. Stir in 1 egg yolk and enough cold water to make a soft dough. Wrap in foil and chill 30 minutes. Roll out and use to line a round 9-inch springform pan; chill again. Heat oven to 375°F. Melt 3 ounces semisweet chocolate with 4 tablespoons unsweetened cocoa powder and 2 tablespoons butter in a bowl over hot water; leave to cool slightly. Cream 6 tablespoons butter with 1 cup unpacked soft brown sugar and slowly beat in 3 eggs. Stir in ⅔ cup light cream and the cooled chocolate mix. Pour into the crust. Bake 35 to 45 minutes until almost firm in the center; leave to cool on a wire rack. Whip ⅔ cup heavy cream to peaks. Spread it over the pie and grate 1 ounce semisweet chocolate over the top.

Banoffee tart

Serves 6 to 8

Crush 1 cup each ginger cookies and graham crackers in a plastic bag with a rolling pin as finely as possible. Mix 1 stick butter with the crumbs and 1 teaspoon apple pie spice. Using a spoon, press into the bottom of a loose-bottomed 7 to 8-inch tart pan lined with plastic wrap; chill to set.

Melt 1 stick butter in a pan. Add 1¾ cups condensed milk and bring to a boil, stirring all the time or it will start to burn. Lower the heat and simmer 5 to 6 minutes, slowly stirring, until it is light golden color. Remove from the heat and beat in 2 tablespoons heavy cream; leave to cool.

Pour the caramel on top of the crumb crust. Peel and slice 4 to 6 bananas and arrange half on top of the caramel. Put another layer of banana on top. Using a sifter, sprinkle with unsweetened cocoa powder; chill. When ready to serve, whip 1¼ cups heavy cream. Spoon on top, dust with more cocoa powder, and serve.

Hot Stuff

The warm embrace of baked and steamed desserts

Lemon and almond cake

Serves 8 to 10

¾ cup butter, softened, plus extra for
  greasing
¾ cup plus 2 tbsp. sugar
3 eggs
1 cup plus 2 tbsp. self-rising flour
20 blanched almonds, finely ground
grated peel and juice of 1 lemon
½ tsp. almond extract
to finish
2 lemons
2 tbsp. honey

1 Heat the oven to 325°F. Grease an 8-inch
springform pan and line the base with waxed
paper.
2 Place the cake ingredients in a large bowl. Mix
well and beat 2 to 3 minutes until light and fluffy.
3 Spoon the batter into the cake pan and smooth
the top. Pare the peel and pith from the lemons.
Thinly slice the lemons. Arrange on top of cake.
4 Bake 50 to 60 minutes until golden and firm.
Leave to cool in the cake pan 5 minutes. Release
the sides and leave to cool a few minutes longer
on a wire rack.
5 Warm the honey and brush it over the warm
cake before serving.

Variation:
Simply substitute orange peel and juice for the
lemon, and oranges for the lemons on top, to
make an orange and almond cake.

(See picture on previous page)

Golden Apricot-Almond Shortcake makes the sunniest of desserts, opposite.

Apricot-almond shortcake

Serves 4

6 tbsp. butter or margarine, plus
  extra for greasing
1 cup plus 2 tbsp. self-rising flour
⅓ cup superfine sugar
1 egg, plus 1 extra yolk
for the filling
20 blanched almonds, finely ground
⅓ cup plus 2 tbsp. superfine sugar
grated peel and juice of 1 orange
1 egg white
14 ounces canned apricot halves in
  their juice
confectioners' sugar, for dusting

1 Heat the oven to 375°F and grease a loose-
bottomed 8-inch tart pan or pie plate. Put the
flour and sugar in a bowl and rub in the butter or
margarine until the mixture has the consistency
of fine bread crumbs.
2 Make a well in the center. Stir in the whole egg
and the extra yolk to make a soft dough. Using
lightly floured hands, press out the dough into the
prepared pan or pie plate.
3 Make the filling: Mix together the almonds, ¼
cup of the sugar, the orange peel, and egg white.
Spread evenly over the shortcake. Drain the
apricots, reserving the juice; arrange the apricots
on the filling. Bake 25 to 30 minutes until lightly
golden and firm to the touch.

4 Place the orange and apricot juices in a pan
with the remaining sugar. Boil rapidly until
reduced by half. Brush over the warm shortcake
and dust with sifted confectioners' sugar.
5 Serve warm, with the remaining syrup if you
like.

Variations:
* Add a spoonful of grated orange or lemon peel
to the dough for extra flavor.
* Replace half the orange juice in the filling with a
similar quantity of orange-flavored liqueur. This
gives the cake a degree of sophistication.

Lemon and lime pudding

This tangy pudding separates during cooking to make a light, cakelike topping with a delicious sauce underneath.

Serves 6

7 tbsp. unsalted butter, softened, plus
   extra for greasing
¾ cup plus 2 tbsp. superfine sugar
finely grated peel and juice of
   3 lemons
finely grated peel and juice of 1 lime
4 large eggs, separated
⅓ cup all-purpose flour
7 tbsp. milk
confectioners' sugar, for dusting
cream, to serve

1 Heat the oven to 350°F. Grease a 6-cup, deep baking dish suitable for serving from. Cream together the butter and sugar until light and fluffy. Stir in the lemon and lime peels and juice, and egg yolks; the mixture will curdle at this stage, but don't worry. Beat in the flour and milk.

2 In a separate bowl, beat the egg whites until soft peaks form. Stir one-quarter of the egg whites into the batter to lighten; gently fold in the remainder.

3 Spoon into the prepared dish. Stand the dish in a roasting pan with enough water to come 1 inch up the sides of the dish. Bake 30 to 35 minutes until risen with a pale golden crust.

4 Dust with sifted confectioners' sugar. Serve warm with cream for pouring over the top.

Pineapple puddings

These puddings are delicious served with a coconut-flavored custard sauce.

Makes 4

1 tbsp. sugar
7 ounces canned pineapple rings in
   their own juice
2 pieces preserved ginger in syrup
4 tbsp. margarine or butter, softened
1/3 cup packed light Barbados sugar
1 large egg
1/2 cup self-rising flour
toasted flaked coconut, to serve

1 Heat the oven to 350°F. Line the bottoms of four 3/4-cup ramekins with waxed paper. In a heavy-bottomed pan, dissolve the sugar in 2 tablespoons water. Boil until golden, without stirring, and pour into the ramekins.
2 Cut 2 of the pineapple rings in half and place a piece in each dish. Quarter one piece of the ginger and place a piece in the middle of each pineapple half. Chop the remaining pineapple and ginger.
3 Beat together the margarine or butter and sugar until pale and fluffy. Beat in the egg. Fold in the flour. Stir in the chopped pineapple and ginger. Spoon into the ramekins and smooth the surfaces. Stand the ramekins in a roasting pan with 3/4 inch water. Bake 25 to 30 minutes until golden.
4 Run a round-bladed knife around the edge of the puddings and turn them out onto individual plates; discard the paper. Sprinkle with toasted flaked coconut to serve.

Fudge apples with orange layered top

The fudgy apples are submerged beneath a fresh orange mixture that divides into a rich custard and the lightest cakelike top.

Serves 6

7 tbsp. butter
6 cups peeled, cored, and chopped
   cooking apples
heaped 2 tbsp. light Barbados sugar
1/2 cup superfine sugar
3 extra-large eggs
finely grated peel and juice of 2 small
   oranges
heaped 2 tbsp. self-rising flour
2/3 cup milk
pinch of salt
1/2 tsp. cream of tartar
whipped cream, to serve

1 Melt half of the butter in a skillet. Stir in the apples and muscovado sugar, and fry over high heat, stirring continuously, about 2 minutes. Transfer to a 7- to 8-inch soufflé dish—a glass baking one is best because it shows off the layers when it is served. Leave to cool.
2 Heat the oven to 350°F. Place the remaining butter in a bowl with the superfine sugar and beat until light and fluffy. Separate the eggs and add the yolks to the mixture. Beat in the orange peel and juice. Sift in the flour and slowly add the milk, beating until the batter is smooth.
3 Beat the egg whites with the salt and cream of tartar until soft peaks form. Using a large metal spoon, fold into the orange batter.
4 Pour on top of the apples. Bake 40 to 50 minutes. Serve hot or cool with whipped cream.

Fruity baked cheesecake

Serves 6

12 graham crackers, crushed
4 tbsp. butter, softened
$\frac{1}{2}$ cup seedless raisins or golden
 raisins
grated peel and juice of 1 lemon
2 cups mascarpone cheese
$\frac{1}{2}$ cup sugar
2 egg yolks, beaten
2 tbsp. cornstarch
$\frac{3}{4}$ cup plus 2 tbsp. sour cream

1 Heat the oven to 400°F. Grease an 8-inch springform cake pan and line with waxed paper. Place the crushed crackers and butter in a bowl and mix until well combined. Transfer to the cake pan and press down into the bottom to make a crust. Bake 7 minutes; leave to cool.
2 Put the raisins or golden raisins and lemon juice in a small pan and simmer 5 minutes; drain well and set aside. In a large bowl beat together the mascarpone cheese and sugar until smooth. Stir the egg yolks into the mascarpone with the lemon peel, cornstarch, sour cream, and fruit.
3 Pour the batter into the prepared cake pan and

smooth the surface. Bake 45 to 50 minutes until golden. Leave to cool completely on a wire rack. Remove from the cake pan to serve.

Variations:
* Add more flavor to the crumb crust with $\frac{1}{2}$ teaspoon ground cinnamon, $\frac{1}{2}$ teaspoon grated orange or lemon peel, or 2 tablespoons cocoa powder.
* While the cheesecake is still warm, sprinkle a little ground cinnamon and/or nutmeg over, followed by a good dusting of confectioners' sugar.

The rugged terrain of Fruity Baked Cheesecake invites the mining of a mouthwatering interior, opposite.

Apricot and pecan cheesecakes

Makes 4

for the crumb crusts
8 graham crackers, crushed
$\frac{1}{3}$ cup pecans, finely ground
3 tbsp. unsalted butter, melted
for the filling
$\frac{3}{4}$ cup plus 2 tbsp. cream cheese
6 tbsp. crème fraîche or sour cream
2 tbsp. superfine sugar
a few drops vanilla extract
grated peel and juice of $\frac{1}{2}$ lemon
2 to 3 fresh apricots, pitted and
 quartered
3 tbsp. apricot jam

1 Heat the oven to 375°F. Make the crumb crusts: Place the crushed crackers, pecans, and butter in a bowl and stir until combined. Press the mixture firmly into the bottom and up the sides of four loose-bottomed 3$\frac{1}{2}$-inch tart pans. Bake 7 to 10 minutes just until the crumb crusts start to color; leave to cool.
2 Place the cream cheese, crème fraîche or sour cream, sugar, vanilla extract, lemon peel, and most of the lemon juice in a bowl and beat until smooth.
3 Remove the crumb crusts from the tart pans. Spoon in the cheesecake batter. Cover and chill for at least 2 hours until firm.
4 Scatter the apricot quarters on top of the

cheesecakes. Warm the jam in a pan with the remaining lemon juice. Brush the fruit with this glaze; leave to cool and chill again before serving.

Variations:
* Instead of fresh apricots, use ready-to-eat dried apricots plumped in a little fruit liqueur or juice.
* Try adding a thin layer of good-quality apricot jam between the crumb crust and the filling.

Baked blueberry cheesecake

This is best made a day in advance to let the flavors develop.

Serves 8

for the crumb crust

3 tbsp. butter, plus extra for greasing
8 graham crackers
¼ cup pecans
1 ounce semisweet chocolate, broken
  into pieces

for the filling

1 cup plus 2 tbsp. curd cheese or
  cottage cheese
1 cup plus 2 tbsp. cream cheese
grated peel of 1 lemon
juice of ½ lemon
2 eggs
½ cup superfine sugar
seeds of 1 vanilla bean
12 ounces fresh blueberries
1 tbsp. all-purpose flour

1 Make the crumb crust: Butter a 9-inch springform round cake pan. Place the graham crackers and the pecans in a food processor and process until fine. (Or chop the nuts and crush the crackers with a rolling pin.) Melt the butter and chocolate in a small bowl set over a pan of simmering water. Stir this into the crumb mixture. Spread over the bottom of the cake pan; chill.

2 Heat the oven to 350°F. Make the filling: Strain the curd and cream cheeses into a bowl. Add the lemon peel and juice, the eggs, sugar, and the vanilla seeds. Beat until the batter is smooth.

3 Toss the blueberries in the flour; fold them into the batter. Pour into the pan. Bake 35 minutes, or until just set. Turn off the oven, leave the door ajar, and leave the cheesecake to cool completely in the oven. Chill for a few hours or, preferably, overnight before serving.

Raisin and vanilla cheesecake

Serves 6 to 8

for the pastry crust
7 tbsp. butter, plus extra for greasing
1 cup plus 3 tbsp. all-purpose flour
6 tbsp. superfine sugar

for the filling
4 tbsp. unsalted butter, softened
7 tbsp. superfine sugar
2 cups curd cheese or cottage cheese
3 eggs
1 tsp. vanilla extract
1/4 cup cornstarch
2/3 cup thick plain yogurt
3/4 cup seedless raisins
confectioners' sugar and ground
   cinnamon, for sprinkling

1 Heat the oven to 325°F. Lightly grease an 8-inch springform cake pan and line the bottom with waxed paper. Make the crust: Sift the flour into a bowl. Cut the butter into small pieces and rub it into the flour using your fingertips until the mixture has the consistency of fine bread crumbs. Stir in the sugar. Sprinkle the mixture evenly over the bottom of the pan. Press down lightly with the back of a spoon. Bake 20 minutes.

2 Meanwhile, make the filling: Beat the butter and sugar until light and fluffy. Beat in the curd cheese. Beat in the eggs, one at a time. Stir in the vanilla, cornstarch, yogurt, and raisins.

3 Set the cake pan on a baking sheet and pour in the filling. Bake 50 to 60 minutes until firm around the edge; leave to cool in the turned off oven with the door ajar.

4 When the cheesecake is cool, chill it until ready to serve. Sprinkle with sifted confectioners' sugar and cinnamon.

Orange-chocolate cheesecake

7 tbsp. butter, softened, plus extra for
   greasing
1/2 cup superfine sugar
2 cups cream cheese
2 eggs, separated
finely grated peel of 2 oranges
20 blanched almonds, finely ground
4 tbsp. all-purpose flour, sifted
2/3 cup bittersweet chocolate morsels
confectioners' sugar and unsweetened
   cocoa powder, to decorate

1 Heat the oven to 350°F and lightly grease an 8-inch springform cake pan. Beat the butter with the sugar until pale and fluffy.

2 Beat in the cream cheese, the egg yolks, orange peel, almonds, and flour until smooth. Beat the egg whites until stiff peaks form. Using a large metal spoon, fold them into the batter. Lightly fold in the chocolate morsels.

3 Spoon the batter into the prepared cake pan. Bake 50 to 60 minutes until golden brown, firm to the touch, and coming away from the side of the pan. (If the cheesecake starts to color too fast, cover it loosely with a double layer of waxed

paper.) Leave to cool in the cake pan about 1 hour on a wire rack.

4 Carefully remove the cheesecake from the cake pan. Dust the top of the cheesecake lightly with sifted confectioners' sugar and dust the middle with cocoa powder, or use a template to make a decorative pattern. Serve cut into slices.

Variation:

For an intriguing reversal, color the cheesecake batter with 2 tablespoons unsweetened cocoa powder and add white chocolate morsels.

New Orleans bread pudding with bourbon sauce

Serves 8

4 tbsp. butter, plus extra for
  greasing
1 ¼ cups light cream
1 ¼ cups milk
1 vanilla bean
½ cup superfine sugar
4 eggs, beaten
1 tbsp. bourbon or Irish whiskey
1 tsp. ground cinnamon
16 thin slices French bread
¾ cup raisins
¼ to ½ cup pecans, chopped
for the bourbon sauce
1 tsp. cornstarch
⅔ cup light cream
2 tbsp. sugar
2 tbsp. bourbon or Irish whiskey

1 Heat oven to 350°F and butter a shallow baking dish that is suitable for serving from. Pour the cream and milk into a pan. Split the vanilla bean along its length, scrape out seeds, and chop. Add bean and seeds to milk. Heat slowly until just boiling. Take off heat, cover, and leave 10 minutes.
2 Beat together the sugar and eggs until frothy. Beat in warm milk mixture. Stir in the bourbon and half the cinnamon. Spread both sides of each slice of bread with butter; arrange slices in dish so they are slightly overlapping. Sprinkle with raisins. Strain the custard sauce over the bread, making sure it is evenly soaked; let stand 10 minutes.
3 Sprinkle the pecans and remaining cinnamon over the top of the pudding. Bake 40 to 45 minutes until the custard has set and the top looks crisp and golden.
4 Make the sauce: Blend the cornstarch to a paste with a little of the cream. Place in a small pan and stir in the remaining cream, sugar, and bourbon. Heat slowly, stirring, until slightly thicker. Simmer 2 to 3 minutes before serving with the pudding.

Louisiana bread pudding

This fragrant spicy version of the old favorite has the texture of a very moist fruit cake. Look for dried cranberries in the dried fruit section of your supermarket—they soak up the milk well and add a delicious sweetness to this recipe.

Serves 6

1 stick butter, melted, plus extra
   for greasing
1 pound whole wheat bread, crusts
   removed
2½ cups milk
¾ cup unpacked soft dark brown
   sugar
4 tsp. apple pie spice
2 large eggs, beaten
2 cups mixed dried fruit, such as
   currants, cranberries, raisins, golden
   raisins, and candied peel
grated peel and juice of 1 orange
½ tsp. freshly grated nutmeg
2 tbsp. brown sugar
crème fraîche or sour cream, maple
   syrup, and cinnamon sticks, to serve
   (optional)

1 Heat the oven to 350°F. Grease a 10 x 5 x 2½-inch cake pan or a 5-cup baking dish and line the bottom with waxed paper. Tear the bread into small pieces and put in a bowl with the milk; leave to stand for 30 minutes. Beat until smooth.
2 Beat in the butter, sugar, apple pie spice, eggs, dried fruit, and orange peel and juice. Pour into the prepared cake pan or dish. Sprinkle some freshly grated nutmeg and brown sugar over. Bake 1¼ hours until risen and a skewer inserted into the center comes out clean. Turn out onto a serving platter and remove the lining paper.
3 Serve warm or at room temperature, with crème fraîche or sour cream, maple syrup, and cinnamon sticks, if you like.

Brown bread pudding

Serves 4

8 slices whole wheat bread
2 tbsp. butter or sunflower oil
   margarine
2 tbsp. marmalade
¾ cup mixed dried fruit
2 eggs
1¼ cups 2-percent milk
1 tsp. ground cinnamon
pinch of freshly grated nutmeg
1 tbsp. light Barbados sugar

1 Heat the oven to 400°F. Spread the slices of bread with the butter or margarine; sandwich them together with the marmalade. Cut off the crusts and slice into triangles; arrange in a greased quiche dish and scatter the dried fruit over.
2 Beat together the eggs, milk, cinnamon, and nutmeg. Strain over the pudding. Sprinkle with the sugar. Bake 25 to 30 minutes until crisp and golden. Serve hot or warm.

Variation:
Use any combination of dried fruit for this recipe, and all kinds of sweet breads work equally well; try loaf, brioche or currant bread.

Roasted pear bundles with ginger and caramel sauce

Makes 4

for the crystallized ginger
1 cup superfine sugar
7 ounces fresh ginger, peeled
  and thinly sliced

for the pears
7 tbsp. butter
½ cup superfine sugar, plus extra
  for sprinkling
3 pears, cored and cut into 8 wedges
2 tsp. fresh lemon juice
eight 8-inch square sheets phyllo
  pastry dough, thawed if frozen
confectioners' sugar, for dusting
mint sprigs, to decorate
vanilla ice cream, to serve (optional)

for the sauce
5 ounces fresh ginger, peeled
  and finely grated
1 cup plus 2 tbsp. cream
¼ cup superfine sugar

1 Make the crystallized ginger: Dissolve the sugar in ¾ cup plus 2 tablespoons water, stirring. Bring to a boil. Add the ginger slices and poach in the syrup 30 minutes.
2 Heat the oven to 230°F. Spread the drained ginger slices on a nonstick baking sheet. Bake about 2 hours until light brown and crisp; remove and leave to cool. Increase the oven setting to 375°F.
3 Cook the pears: Melt 4 tablespoons of the butter in a skillet. Add sugar. Just before it turns a caramel color, add the pears and cook 8 to 10 minutes, coating them in the caramel. Stir in the lemon juice and half the crystallized ginger; reserve the rest for decoration. Remove from the heat and leave to cool.

4 Melt the remaining butter in a small pan. Brush a sheet of phyllo dough with melted butter and sprinkle with a little sugar. Lay another sheet on top. Place about 6 pear slices and some juice in the center. Brush the dough edges with melted butter; draw up the corners to make a bundle. Place on a lightly oiled baking sheet and brush with butter. Make 3 more bundles in the same way. Bake 10 to 12 minutes until golden.
5 Meanwhile, make the sauce: Wrap the ginger in a clean cloth and squeeze the juice into a small bowl. In a pan, slowly heat the cream to just below the boiling point. In a

separate pan, slowly heat the sugar and 3 tablespoons water until the sugar dissolves. Increase the heat and simmer until mixture turns light golden. Slowly stir in the hot cream and the ginger juice. Bring to a boil; remove from the heat and strain.

6 Place a pear bundle on each serving plate. Dust with sifted confectioners' sugar and decorate with a mint sprig. Drizzle the sauce around and scatter around some crystallized ginger. Serve plain or with vanilla ice cream.

Baked apples

Makes 4

2 Golden Delicious apples, cut across
   in half and cored
2 tbsp. butter, plus extra for greasing
2 tbsp. light brown sugar
for the filling
1 small tart, crisp apple like Granny Smith
good pinch of ground ginger
1 egg yolk
1 tbsp. heavy cream
1 tbsp. brandy

1 Heat the oven to 400°F. Arrange the apple halves in a buttered baking dish and sprinkle half the brown sugar over. Bake 7 to 10 minutes, or until the apples are partly cooked.
2 Make the filling: Peel and core the Granny Smith apple; grate it into a small bowl. Stir in the ground ginger, egg yolk, heavy cream, and brandy.
3 Divide the grated apple filling between the 4 apple halves to cover their cut surfaces completely. Sprinkle with the remaining sugar and dot with pieces of butter.
4 Bake 15 minutes, or until the surface is golden and bubbling.

Baked stuffed pears

Makes 6

¾ cup ricotta cheese or low-fat cream
   cheese
1½ cups grated Wensleydale or cheddar
   cheese
seeds from 1 cardamom pod, crushed
3 tbsp. honey
3 tbsp. unsalted butter
6 ripe pears
2 tbsp. pear or apple juice
1 tbsp. brandy
fromage blanc, for decorating

1 Heat the oven to 400°F. Beat the ricotta or low-fat cheese with the Wensleydale or cheddar cheese, cardamom seeds, honey, and 2 tablespoons of the butter until smooth.
2 Peel, halve, and core the pears. Press the cheese filling into the hollowed centers. Place the pears in a baking dish just big enough to fit them snugly together in a single layer. Dot over the remaining butter and pour in the pear or apple juice and brandy.

3 Cover with foil and bake 30 to 35 minutes until the pears are tender.
4 Place the pears under a preheated hot broiler 3 to 4 minutes until they turn golden.
5 Serve hot with a sauce of the pan juices and decorated with fromage blanc.

Variation:
Try this with some dolcelatte or Roquefort cheese in place of the Wensleydale.

Peach popovers

Makes 4

½ cup all-purpose flour
1 egg
½ cup 2% milk
a little butter
7 ounces canned peach slices packed in
    natural juice, drained and cut in half
    lengthwise
1 tbsp. sugar
¼ tsp. grated lemon peel

1 Heat the oven to 425°F. Sift the flour into a
bowl. Make a well in the center and break in the
egg. Add half of the milk and gradually stir into
the flour. Beat the batter until smooth. Beat in the
remaining milk; the batter should have the
consistency of light cream.
2 Place a little butter in 4 cups on a muffin pan.
Heat in the oven 1 minute until the butter melts;
do not let it burn.
3 Pour the batter into the muffin cups and add the
peaches, divided equally. Bake 20 to 25 minutes
until risen and golden brown.
4 Meanwhile, mix together the sugar and lemon
peel. Sprinkle over each popover just before
serving.

Almond and orange baked apples

Makes 4

4 eating apples
grated peel and juice of 1 orange
4 tbsp. store-bought mincemeat
1 egg white, lightly beaten
15 blanched almonds, finely ground
2 tbsp. sugar
custard sauce (see page 40) or
    yogurt, to serve

1 Heat the oven to 400°F. Peel and core the
apples; brush with orange juice. Fill the center of
each apple with mincemeat, making sure you pack
it down well.
2 Put the egg white into a small bowl. Mix the
almonds, sugar, and orange peel in a separate
bowl. Coat the apples in the egg white followed
by the almond mix until they are completely
covered.
3 Place the apples in a buttered baking dish. Bake
50 to 60 minutes until the apples are tender and
the coating is crisp and golden brown.
4 Serve hot with custard sauce or yogurt.

Peach clafoutis

The clafoutis is a classic French fruit dessert. A cross between a plump pancake and a pudding, it is easy to prepare and makes an ideal family dessert served warm.

Serves 6

3 extra-large eggs
1 cup all-purpose flour
heaping ¾ cup confectioners' sugar,
    plus extra for dusting
1¼ cups 2% milk
1 tsp. vanilla extract
butter, for greasing
14 ounces canned peaches packed
    in natural juice, drained
grated peel of 1 lemon

1 Heat the oven to 375°F. In a bowl, beat together the eggs, flour, sugar, milk, and vanilla extract.
2 Cover the bottom of a greased 8-inch baking dish with the peaches and sprinkle the lemon peel over. Pour in the batter. Bake 35 minutes, or until the batter is firm.
3 Dust with sifted confectioners' sugar. Serve warm.

The clafoutis treatment works equally well with fresh peaches, or try the classic version with black cherries, unpitted for fuller flavor.

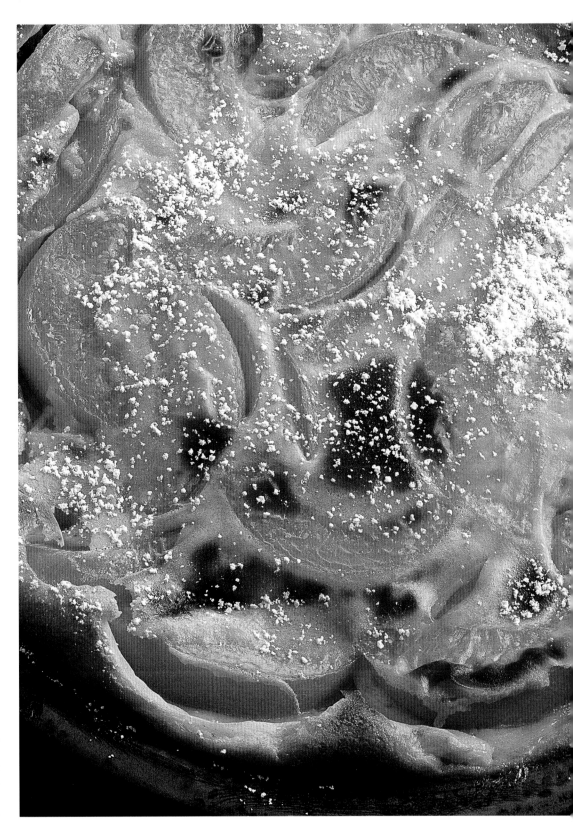

Master class: Making steamed puddings

Orange marmalade steamed pudding

Serves 4

7 tbsp. unsalted butter, softened, plus extra
   for greasing
2 tbsp. golden syrup (see page 84) or
   maple syrup
grated peel and juice of ½ orange
½ cup superfine sugar
3 eggs, lightly beaten
3 tbsp. orange marmalade
½ cup plus 1 tbsp. self-rising flour
1 tsp. baking powder
1 tsp. cinnamon
1½ cups fresh white bread crumbs
cream or custard sauce, to serve

1 Lightly grease a 5-cup heatproof bowl. Mix
the golden syrup with the orange peel and
juice. Pour and spoon into the bottom of the
bowl (2).
2 In a large mixing bowl, beat together the
butter and sugar until light and fluffy. Beat in
the eggs, a little at a time, until incorporated.
Stir in the orange marmalade.
3 Sift together the flour, baking powder, and
cinnamon. Using a large metal spoon, fold into
the creamed mixture. Fold in the bread
crumbs (3).
4 Spoon the batter into the prepared bowl.
Cover the top with 2 layers of waxed paper
and a layer of foil (4), all three pleated across
the middle; this lets the pudding expand
during cooking.
5 Tie securely with string around the top of
the bowl and secure an extra length of string
to form a handle. Place in a steamer, or sit on
an upturned saucer in a large saucepan. Pour
in enough boiling water to reach halfway up
the sides of the bowl. Cover with a tight-fitting
lid. Steam 2 hours; the water should simmer
gently. Check regularly to make sure the pan

doesn't become dry and only top up with
boiling water.
6 Carefully lift out the pudding bowl (5 & 6).
Remove the foil and waxed paper from the
pudding; protect your hands from the steam.

The pudding should be firm to the touch. Test
with a skewer—it should come out clean
when inserted in the center. Leave the
pudding to cool slightly before unmolding.
7 Serve hot with cream or custard sauce.

Individual chocolate and hazelnut steamed puddings

You can use deep ramekins or metal dariole molds for this recipe. Ovenproof teacups are also suitable.

Makes 6

7 tbsp. unsalted butter,
softened, plus extra for greasing
¾ cup chopped hazelnuts, toasted
4 tbsp. maple syrup
3½ ounces semisweet chocolate,
broken into small pieces
⅔ cup packed light Barbados sugar
3 eggs, lightly beaten
½ cup plus 1 tbsp. self-rising flour
1 tsp. baking powder
1 tbsp. unsweetened cocoa powder
1½ cups fresh white bread crumbs
extra maple syrup and cream or
custard, to serve

1 Grease 6 ramekins or dariole molds. Mix 3 tablespoons of the toasted hazelnuts with the maple syrup. Place 1 tablespoonful of the mixture into the bottom of each mold.
2 Place 3 ounces of the chocolate in a small heatproof bowl. Set the bowl over a pan of gently simmering water and heat until the chocolate melts.
3 Beat together the butter and sugar until light and fluffy. Gradually beat in the eggs. Sift together the flour, baking powder, and cocoa powder. Using a large metal spoon, fold into butter and sugar. Stir in the melted chocolate, the remaining chocolate pieces, the remaining hazelnuts, and the bread crumbs.

4 Spoon the batter into the ramekins or dariole molds until each is two thirds full. Cover the tops with foil. Stand them in a steamer or in a large saucepan. Pour in boiling water to reach halfway up the sides of the molds.
5 Cover the pan and simmer 30 to 40 minutes until the puddings rise to the top of the molds. Remove the foil; the puddings should be firm to the touch.
6 Unmold onto individual plates. Serve hot with extra maple syrup and cream or custard sauce.

Opposite: **The unholy trinity (clockwise from the top left): Pear and Almond Steamed Pudding; Ginger, Lemon, and Honey Steamed Pudding; and Individual Chocolate and Hazelnut Steamed Puddings.**

Ginger, lemon, and honey steamed pudding

Serves 6

7 tbsp. unsalted butter,
softened, plus extra for greasing
2 tbsp. honey
2-inch piece preserved ginger, finely
chopped, plus 1 tbsp. of the syrup
1 lemon, peel and pith removed,
thinly sliced
½ cup superfine sugar
3 eggs, lightly beaten
½ cup plus 1 tbsp. self-rising flour
1 tsp. baking powder
1½ cups fresh white bread crumbs
1 tbsp. ground ginger
cream or custard sauce, to serve

1 Grease the inside of a 5-cup heatproof bowl. Mix together the honey and ginger syrup. Pour into the bottom of the bowl. Press the lemon slices into the syrup on the bottom and up the sides of the bowl.
2 In a large mixing bowl, beat together the butter and sugar until light and fluffy. Beat in the eggs, a little at a time, until incorporated.
3 Sift together the flour and baking powder. Using a large metal spoon, fold into the creamed mixture. Fold in the bread crumbs, preserved ginger, and ground ginger.
4 Cover and steam as described in the master class recipe on the previous pages. Serve warm, with cream or custard.

Pear and almond steamed pudding

Serves 6

7 tbsp. unsalted butter,
   softened, plus extra for greasing
2 tbsp. raspberry jam
2 pears, peeled, cored, and chopped
1 tbsp. lemon juice
½ cup superfine sugar
3 eggs, lightly beaten
½ cup plus 1 tbsp. self-rising flour
1 tbsp. baking powder
1¼ cups fresh white bread crumbs
½ cup slivered almonds, toasted
cream or custard sauce, to serve

1 Lightly grease a 5-cup heatproof bowl. Spoon the jam into the bottom. Toss the chopped pears in the lemon juice; set aside.
2 In a large mixing bowl, beat together the butter and sugar until light and fluffy. Beat in the eggs, a little at a time, until incorporated.
3 Sift together the flour and baking powder. Using a large metal spoon, fold into the creamed mixture. Fold in the bread crumbs, pears, and almonds.
4 Spoon the batter into the prepared bowl. Cover and steam following the directions in the master class recipe on pages 130 and 131. Serve with cream or custard sauce.

Variations:
* You can use any type of good fruit jam in the bottom of the bowl. A fine-cut marmalade will also work well.
* Toss the pears in a nut- or fruit-flavored liqueur instead of the lemon juice.

Gingered fruit steamed pudding

Serves 8

for the fruit filling
4 tbsp. butter, cut into small cubes,
   plus extra for greasing
7 ounces canned pineapple chunks
   packed in natural juice
2 bananas
2 ripe pears
⅓ cup packed light Barbados sugar
for the batter
⅔ cup packed light Barbados sugar
7 tbsp. butter
2 eggs, beaten
1 cup plus 2 tbsp. whole wheat
   self-rising flour
1½ tsp. baking powder
2 tsp. ground ginger
3½ ounces crystallized ginger or
   drained preserved ginger, chopped
custard sauce, to serve

1 Butter a 7½-cup heatproof bowl. Put a circle of waxed paper in the bottom. Make the fruit filling: Drain the pineapple; reserve 3 tablespoons of the juice. Peel and slice the bananas. Peel, core, and chop the pears. Mix the fruit with the sugar and butter. Spoon half of this mixture into the bowl.
2 Make the pudding batter: Beat the sugar and butter until light and fluffy. Beat in the eggs, a little at a time. Fold in the flour, baking powder, and ground and crystallized ginger. Stir in the reserved pineapple juice. Spoon half the batter into the bowl and smooth the surface. Spoon the remaining fruit mixture over the top. Top with the remaining batter and smooth the top.
3 Cover and steam as in the master class recipe on pages 130 and 131. Steam 2 hours until risen and firm. Leave to cool for 10 minutes. Unmold and remove the paper. Serve with custard sauce.

Apricot, pecan, and pear steamed pudding

Serves 8

for the topping
4 tbsp. butter, plus extra for greasing
1/3 cup packed light Barbados sugar
1/2 cup pecan halves, roughly
  chopped
3/4 cup chopped ready-to-eat dried
  apricots

for the batter
1 3/4 cups plus 2 tbsp. self-rising flour
7 tbsp. butter, cut into small cubes
8 1/2 tbsp. light Barbados sugar
1 pear, grated
2 eggs, beaten
1/2 cup milk
heavy cream or ice cream, to serve

1 Make the topping: Combine all the
ingredients. Spoon into a buttered 7-cup
heatproof bowl.
2 Make the pudding batter: Put the flour in a
bowl. Add the butter and rub in with your
fingertips until the mixture has the consistency of
fine bread crumbs. Stir in the sugar and pear. Add
the eggs and milk and mix until a soft batter
forms. Spoon over the topping and smooth the
surface.
3 Cover and steam as in the master class recipe
on pages 130 and 131. Steam 1 1/2 to 2 hours until
firm to the touch. Unmold and serve with cream
or ice cream.

Seven-cup steamed pudding with a butterscotch sauce

Serves 4

1 cup seedless raisins or dried currants
1 cup golden raisins
1 cup self-rising flour
1 cup grated beef suet
1 cup fresh bread crumbs
1 cup soft light brown sugar
1 tsp. ground cinnamon
1 tsp. apple pie spice
1 cup milk
1 egg, beaten
butter, for greasing
crème fraîche or sour cream, to serve

for the butterscotch sauce
heaping 1/2 cup packed soft dark brown sugar
4 tbsp. unsalted butter
2/3 cup heavy cream
few drops vanilla extract

1 Combine the dry ingredients. Stir in the milk and egg until well combined. Pour into a buttered 8-cup heatproof bowl. Cover with a double layer of buttered foil, pleated across the center. Secure with string.
2 Place the bowl in a large pan and half fill with boiling water. Bring the water to a boil. Cover and steam 2½ to 3 hours, checking the water level

frequently. When almost ready, heat the oven to 400°F.
3 Make the butterscotch sauce: Heat all of the ingredients in a pan until the sugar dissolves. Bring to a boil and boil 2 to 3 minutes until syrupy.
4 Unmold the pudding onto a heatproof serving dish. Pour over half the sauce. Bake 3 to 4 minutes until the sauce bubbles. Serve with crème fraîche or sour cream and more of the sauce.

The caramelized apples filling the Apple Flapjack Steamed Pudding, opposite, tumble invitingly from their hiding place.

Apple flapjack steamed pudding
The lemon-scented apples are the perfect foil for the sticky, sweet crust. Hot custard sauce is the best accompaniment.

Serves 8

1½ pounds eating apples
1/3 cup packed light brown sugar
grated peel and juice of 1 lemon
1 cup packed dark Barbados sugar
1/2 cup plus 2 tbsp. butter
4 tbsp. golden syrup (see page 84), or light corn syrup
2/3 cup self-rising whole wheat flour
1 tsp. baking powder
3 cups oatmeal
2 tsp. ground cinnamon
2 eggs, beaten
custard sauce, to serve

1 Quarter, peel, and core the apples; cut each quarter into 3 slices. Place in a pan with the brown sugar, lemon peel, and juice. Heat slowly and cook 5 minutes until the apples are just starting to soften. Using a draining spoon, remove from the pan. Boil the sauce until reduced and thickened. Pour the sauce over the apples.
2 Put the Barbados sugar, butter, and syrup into a small pan. Heat slowly until the butter melts; leave to cool slightly. In a mixing bowl, mix together the flour, baking powder, oatmeal, and cinnamon. Make a well in the center. Pour in the melted mixture and the eggs, stirring until a smooth batter forms.
3 Spread two-thirds of the mixture evenly over

the bottom and side of a buttered 7½-cup heatproof bowl. Fill with the apples and spread the remaining batter on the top. Cover and steam as in the master class recipe on pages 130 and 131. Steam 2 hours.
4 Leave to cool in the bowl 10 minutes. Unmold and serve with custard.

Chilling Out

A cool appraisal of frozen desserts

Master class: Making ice cream

Vanilla ice cream

Serves 6
(makes about 3 cups)

1¼ cups whole milk
1 vanilla bean
4 egg yolks
½ cup plus 2 tbsp. superfine sugar
1¼ cups heavy cream

1 Pour the milk into a small pan. Using a sharp knife, split the vanilla bean lengthwise and scrape the seeds into the milk. Cut the pod into several pieces and add to the pan. Slowly bring almost to a boil. Remove the pan from the heat, cover, and leave to infuse at least 15 minutes, but preferably 30 minutes.

2 In a bowl, beat together the egg yolks and sugar about 1 minute until thick and creamy and the batter leaves a distinct trail when the beaters are lifted. Bring the flavored milk back to a boil. Pour it slowly into the beaten eggs, stirring continuously.

3 Pour the custard mixture into a clean, preferably nonstick, pan. Simmer over very low heat, stirring continuously with a wooden spoon until the custard coats the back of the spoon; this will take 8 to 10 minutes. Do not let the custard boil or it will separate.

4 Stand a clean bowl in another bowl filled with ice, or with a mixture of ice and cold water. Strain the custard mixture through a fine strainer into the bowl, pressing down on the vanilla pieces to extract all the flavor; leave to cool about 30 minutes, stirring occasionally to prevent a skin from forming. When completely cool, stir in the cream. Chill at least 3 hours, or overnight if you prefer.

5 Start the ice-cream machine running, then pour in the mixture. (Go to step 6 if you don't have a machine.) Churn until it is thick and has the consistency of softly whipped cream; this will take about 30 minutes, depending on your machine, the coldness of the mixture, and how long your container has been in the freezer. Spoon the ice cream into a freezerproof plastic container, cover, and freeze until firm. Transfer to the refrigerator 30 minutes before serving.

6 If you do not have an ice-cream machine, freeze the bowl of cold or chilled custard about 2 hours until it is firm to about 1 inch from the edge. Remove from the freezer and beat with a wire whisk to break down the ice crystals. Return to the freezer until semifrozen. Beat again. Spoon into a freezerproof container, cover, and freeze again until firm. Freeze up to 2 months.

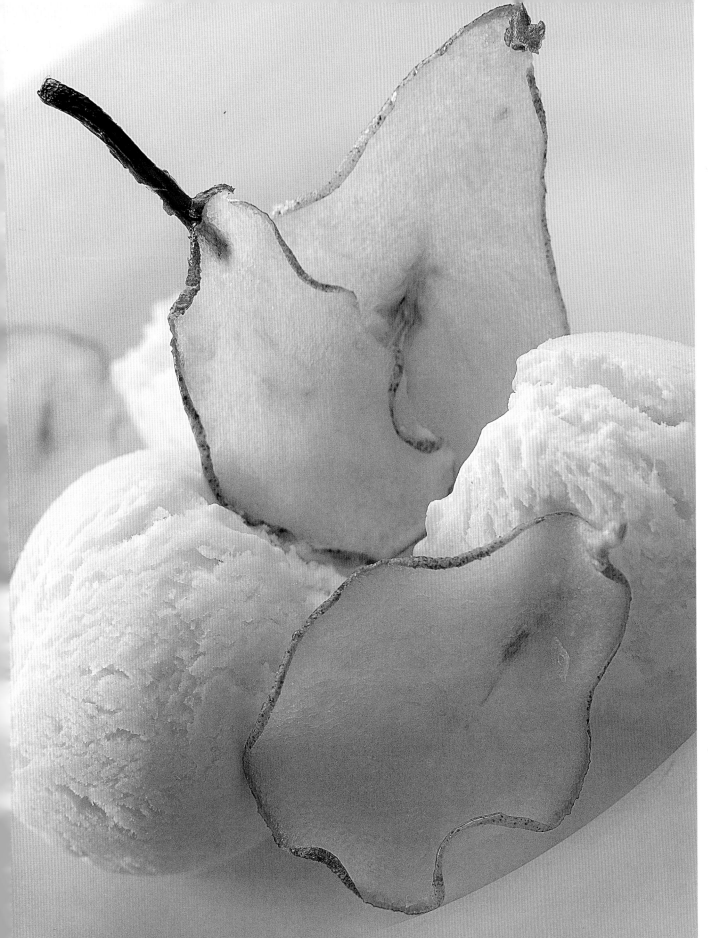

Vanilla Ice Cream with Pear Crisps. The strong, fruity flavor and deliciously crunchy texture of Pear Crisps (page 36) make them the perfect foil for good homemade vanilla ice cream.

141

Crunchy cappuccino ice cream

This is easy to make and great to have in your freezer for a luxuriously rich after-dinner dessert.

Serves 8

3 egg yolks
¾ cup unpacked light Barbados sugar
1¼ cups 2% milk
1 tbsp. instant coffee granules dissolved in 2 tbsp. boiling water, cooled
½ cup Amaretto liqueur
3½ ounces amaretti cookies, lightly crushed
1 cup chocolate-coated coffee beans
1 tsp. unsweetened cocoa powder, plus extra to dust
1 tsp. vanilla extract
2 cups heavy cream
chocolate curls (see page 100), to decorate (optional)

1 Put the egg yolks, sugar, and milk in a heatproof bowl over a pan of simmering water. Beat 5 minutes until pale and thick enough to coat the back of a wooden spoon; do not let the custard boil. Leave to cool.
2 Stir the coffee, liqueur, cookie crumbs, chocolate coffee beans, cocoa powder, and vanilla extract into the cooled custard.
3 In a separate bowl, whip the cream until soft peaks form. Stir into the custard mixture.
4 Spoon into a freezerproof container and freeze. Remove from the freezer after 1 hour and beat. Freeze for another hour; beat again. Cover and freeze until required.
5 Remove from the freezer 15 minutes before serving. Serve, dusted with sifted cocoa powder and decorated with chocolate curls, if you like.

Christmas ice cream

Use any combination of dried fruits you like in this recipe.

Serves 6 to 8

2½ tbsp. sweetened dried cranberries
2 tbsp. chopped dried mango slices
2 tbsp. ready-to-eat dried apricots, chopped
2 tbsp. seedless raisins, chopped
4 tbsp. brandy
2½ cups heavy cream
¼ cup unpacked light Barbados sugar
heaping 1 cup fresh fine whole wheat bread crumbs
2 tbsp. pine nuts
½ tsp. ground cinnamon
fresh cranberries and bay leaves, brushed with a little egg white and dusted with superfine sugar, to decorate (optional)

1 Put the cranberries, mango, apricots, and raisins in a bowl. Stir in the brandy; leave to soak.
2 Meanwhile, beat the cream and 1½ tablespoons of the sugar until thick. Transfer to a freezerproof container and freeze, stirring every 30 minutes, for 2 to 3 hours until almost set.
3 Heat the oven to 400°F. Mix together the remaining sugar with the bread crumbs, pine nuts, and cinnamon. Spread over a baking sheet. Bake 5 to 10 minutes until golden brown and caramelized. Leave to cool. When cool, break up into small pieces.
4 Using a large metal spoon, fold the soaked fruit and bread crumb mixture into the ice cream until well mixed. Freeze 2 hours until set. If you like, you can decorate with "frosted" cranberries and bay leaves.

Atholl brose ice cream

This ice cream is based on a luscious Scottish syllabub-style dessert made from oatmeal, cream, honey, and Scotch whisky.

Serves 12

2½ cups milk
5 egg yolks
¼ cup superfine sugar
4 tbsp. honey, preferably wildflower honey
4 tbsp. Scotch whisky
⅓ cup medium steel-cut oatmeal
¼ cup granulated sugar
1¼ cups heavy cream

1 Bring the milk to just below a boil. In a heatproof and freezerproof bowl, whisk the egg yolks with the superfine sugar until pale and thick. Stir in the hot milk.
2 Place the bowl over a pan of simmering water and stir until the custard coats the back of the spoon, about 30 minutes. Stir in the honey. Leave to cool; stir in the whisky.
3 Freeze the mixture in its bowl 1 hour. Meanwhile, stir the oats and granulated sugar together. Place on a baking sheet and toast under a heated broiler, removing frequently to stir with a fork, until the sugar caramelizes. Break into

large crumbs with a fork. Leave to cool; chill.
4 Whip the cream until soft peaks form. Beat the partially frozen custard to loosen it slightly. Stir in the oats and fold in the cream. Return to the freezer 1 hour.
5 Beat the ice cream again. Transfer to an ice-cream maker or freezerproof container. Freeze until firm.

Strawberry ice cream

Serves 8

2 cups milk
1 vanilla bean, split
6 egg yolks
1/4 cup plus 2 tbsp. superfine sugar
1 3/4 cups heavy cream
1 pound strawberries, hulled, plus
   extra to decorate
juice of 1 lemon
3/4 cup confectioners' sugar
mint sprigs, to decorate

1 Place the milk and vanilla bean in a pan. Bring to a boil. Beat the egg yolks and sugar together until thick and light. Stir in a little boiling milk to blend, then pour it into the pan. Simmer over low heat, stirring; do not let boil. When thick, leave to cool and remove the vanilla bean.

2 Transfer the custard to an ice-cream maker and churn until thick. Add the cream and churn until frozen. Place the ice cream in a freezerproof container and freeze until required. Alternatively, place the cooled custard in a freezerproof container, cover, and freeze, stirring occasionally to prevent any large ice crystals

from forming. When thick, stir in the cream and return to the freezer.

3 Place half of the strawberries in a bowl with the lemon juice and confectioners' sugar; mash with a fork. Roughly chop the remaining strawberries and stir into the mashed mixture. Transfer to an ice-cream maker and churn until thick, or freeze as for the ice cream.

4 Fold the strawberry mixture into the ice cream, leaving it streaky; work quickly to prevent it from becoming too soft. Cover and freeze at least 2 hours. To serve, decorate with more strawberries and mint sprigs.

Raspberry sorbet in strawberry tuiles with dried strawberry slices

If you have any cassis, add a couple of tablespoons to the raspberry purée—it really enhances the flavor.

Serves 8

1 pound raspberries
1 tbsp. honey
2 egg whites
1/2 cup superfine sugar

for the oven-dried strawberry slices

1/2 pound ripe but firm strawberries, hulled
3 tbsp. superfine sugar

for the strawberry tuiles (makes 20 cookies)

2/3 cup blanched almonds, finely ground
3 tbsp. all-purpose flour
1/4 cup plus 1 1/2 tbsp. sugar
1/2 ounce oven-dried strawberry slices (as above), crushed
2 tbsp. butter, melted and cooled, plus extra for the baking sheets
1 egg white, lightly beaten with a fork

(See the picture on page 138)

1 Purée the raspberries with 3/4 cup plus 2 tablespoons water and honey in a food processor or blender. Pass the mixture through a fine strainer.

2 If you have an ice-cream maker, churn the raspberry mixture until it begins to freeze. Alternatively, put it in a freezerproof container and freeze until ice crystals form. Stir to break up the crystals.

3 Put the egg whites and sugar into a clean, greasefree bowl. Place this over a pan of hot water on a medium heat. Beat the mixture until it forms a smooth meringue that can hold its shape, about 5 minutes.

4 Leave the meringue to cool. Fold it into the freezing fruit mixture. Return to the freezer 3 to 4 hours until frozen.

5 Make the oven-dried strawberry slices: Heat the oven to 230°F. Thinly slice the strawberries lengthwise. Arrange a layer in a bowl and sprinkle with a little sugar; repeat until all the slices are used up.

6 Transfer the slices, one at a time, to a nonstick baking sheet; it is important to use nonstick so you can remove the strawberry slices when dry.

7 Bake 1 1/2 hours. Turn the slices over and bake 1

hour longer until dry; leave to cool. These can be stored in an airtight container or jar for up to 4 weeks.

8 Make the strawberry tuiles: In a bowl, mix the almonds, flour, sugar, and dried strawberries. Add the butter and egg white and stir in with a fork. Cover and chill 30 minutes.

9 Heat the oven to 325°F. Butter 3 baking sheets. Place about 20 spoonfuls of mixture on the baking sheets, spaced well apart.

10 Using a piece of plastic wrap to cover the piles of mixture, flatten into circles about 3 inches wide and 1/16 inch thick; remove the plastic wrap. Bake one sheet at a time 8 to 10 minutes until the cookies are golden at the edges.

11 Using a metal spatula, remove the cookies from the baking sheet while hot. Lightly press each one over a rolling pin to curl. Leave to harden for a few minutes; transfer to a wire rack to cool. (These can be stored in an airtight container for up to 2 weeks. If they become slightly soft, crisp them briefly in the oven.)

12 About 30 minutes before you want to serve, transfer the sorbet to the refrigerator. Serve the sorbet nestling in the strawberry tuiles, decorated with the strawberry slices.

Frozen peach yogurt

This custard-based dessert can also be made with pineapple, gooseberries, or nectarines.

Serves 4

3 egg yolks
¾ cup superfine sugar
⅔ cup milk
8 large ripe peaches
3 tbsp. fresh lemon juice
⅔ cup thick plain yogurt
2 tbsp. almond liqueur (optional)

1 Beat together the egg yolks and sugar in a bowl until pale. Heat the milk until almost boiling. Pour the milk into the egg mixture, beating continuously. Return the custard to the pan and simmer, stirring, until thickened; do not let boil. Leave to cool; chill.
2 Peel and pit the peaches. Purée half the peaches with the lemon juice and finely chop the rest. Stir the peach purée, yogurt, and liqueur, if using, into the custard. Pour the mixture into a freezerproof container and freeze until set 1 inch in from the sides.
3 Tip the frozen yogurt into a chilled bowl and beat to break down the ice crystals. Return to the container and freeze for 1 hour longer. Beat again, stirring in the chopped peaches. Return to the freezer until firm.
4 Transfer the frozen yogurt to the refrigerator about 30 minutes before serving to let it soften slightly. Serve with fresh fruit or a raspberry or strawberry coulis made by puréeing the fruit, straining it, and sweetening it with a little sifted confectioners' sugar.

Peach melba swirl

The Frozen Peach Yogurt and Raspberry Sorbet can be combined to spectacular effect for a special party dessert.

Serves 10 to 12

Frozen Peach Yogurt (above)
Raspberry Sorbet (left)

1 Make up one quantity each of Frozen Peach Yogurt and Raspberry Sorbet until both are just firm.
2 Fill a container with alternate scoops of frozen yogurt and sorbet, swirling together. Freeze until firm.
3 Serve in scoops to show off the swirls.

Griddled strawberries with lemon curd ice cream and lemon shortbread

Griddled strawberries coupled with refreshing ice cream and melt-in-your-mouth shortbread are a temptation few can resist!

Serves 4 to 6

for the lemon curd (optional, makes about 3 cups)
1 cup plus 2 tbsp. superfine sugar
2 sticks unsalted butter
finely grated peel and juice of 3 lemons
5 egg yolks

for the ice cream
1 quantity lemon curd as above, or
   3 cups store-bought lemon curd
2 heaped tbsp. crème fraîche
1 heaped tbsp. plain yogurt

for the lemon shortbread
7 tbsp. unsalted butter, plus extra for
   greasing
1/4 cup superfine sugar, plus extra for
   sprinkling if you like
finely grated peel of 1 lemon
1 cup all-purpose flour

for the griddled strawberries
1 pound fresh strawberries
2 tbsp. confectioners' sugar
2 tbsp. butter
fresh mint sprigs, to decorate (optional)

1 If you are making the lemon curd, place the sugar, butter, and lemon juice and peel in a bowl over a pan of simmering water. Stir until melted, then beat vigorously until combined. Beat in the egg yolks and simmer, stirring, 15 to 20 minutes until thick. Pour into a sterilized jar and cover with waxed paper or plastic film. Once cooled, seal tightly and store in the refrigerator. It will keep for up to 2 weeks.

2 Make the ice cream: Stir the lemon curd with the crème fraîche and yogurt. Churn in an ice-cream machine. Alternatively, freeze the mixture in a covered freezerproof container until set about 1 1/4 inches in from the edges. Beat to break down the larger

crystals. Return to the freezer; repeat twice.
3 Make the lemon shortbread: Heat the oven to 350°F. Grease a baking sheet and line it with nonstick baking paper. Beat the butter and sugar until pale and fluffy. Stir in the lemon peel. Sift the flour and work it into the

lemon butter. Using a pastry bag, pipe the mixture on the baking sheet in 12 round or long shapes. Bake 20 minutes until pale golden brown. Transfer the cookies to a wire rack; leave to cool. Sprinkle with sugar, if you like.

4 Make the sauce for the griddled strawberries: Chop 4 or 5 strawberries. Place

them in a pan with 2 teaspoons confectioners' sugar and 3 tablespoons water. Stir over low heat 2 to 3 minutes. Press the mixture through a fine strainer into a bowl.

5 Heat a griddle or skillet over high heat. Brush with the butter. Add the remaining strawberries and sift 1 tablespoon

confectioners' sugar over the top. Cook about 2 minutes. Turn the strawberries over and cook 2 to 3 minutes longer.

6 Serve the griddled strawberries warm with the strawberry sauce, ice cream, and shortbread. Decorate with mint, if you like.

Frozen strawberry-yogurt terrine

Serves 8

1¼ cups heavy cream
¾ cup superfine sugar
1 pound strawberries, hulled, plus
   extra to decorate
1¼ cups thick strawberry yogurt

1 Chill a 9 x 5-inch bread pan in the freezer. Whip half of the cream. Spread three-quarters of it over the bottom and sides of the loaf pan. Return to the freezer and chill the remaining cream.

2 Dissolve the sugar in ¾ cup water in a small pan. Bring to a boil and boil until the temperature reaches 225°F on a candy thermometer. (Or a drop of the syrup dropped in cold water forms a thread when pulled.)

3 Roughly chop half the strawberries. Place them in a food processor or blender with the syrup and process until smooth. (Or mash to a purée, and stir in the syrup.) Add the yogurt. Pour into an ice-cream maker and churn until

thick, or place in a freezerproof container and freeze, stirring occasionally, until thick.

4 Chop the remaining strawberries. Whip the remaining cream (but not the reserved chilled cream). Fold the strawberries and cream into the yogurt mixture. Spoon into the cream-lined pan. Freeze several hours until firm. Spread the reserved chilled cream on top. Return to the freezer until set.

5 Run the tip of a round-bladed knife around the edge of the mold to loosen. Dip the bottom in hot water and invert onto a chilled plate. Smooth the cream with a metal spatula. Decorate with more strawberries and serve at once.

Chocolate and chestnut parfait

Serves 6 to 8

5 ounces amaretti cookies, coarsely
   crushed
4 tbsp. brandy
1⅓ cups canned sweetened chestnut purée
3 ounces bittersweet chocolate, chopped
2 cups heavy cream
for the coating
3½ ounces bittersweet chocolate
3 tbsp. heavy cream
for the decoration
2 ounces bittersweet chocolate
vegetable oil, for greasing
confectioners' sugar, for dusting

1 Mix together the amaretti cookies and brandy in a bowl; leave to soak 10 to 15 minutes until the brandy has soaked into the cookies. Stir in the chestnut purée and the chopped chocolate.

2 Whip the cream until it is stiff. Fold it into the chestnut mixture. Rinse a 1-quart freezerproof bowl with cold water—don't dry it—and fill with the chestnut cream. Freeze 12 hours or overnight, until firm.

3 Break up the chocolate for the coating. Put in a small bowl with the cream and set over a pan of hot water, stirring until a smooth sauce forms. Remove from the heat; leave to cool.

4 Dip the bottom of the bowl quickly into hot

water. Unmold onto a freezerproof plate. Spread quickly with the chocolate coating, swirling it over the top and sides. Return to the freezer until it is firm.

5 Break up the chocolate for the decoration. Place in a bowl over hot water and stir until it melts. Spread over a board lined with lightly oiled foil; leave until just set. Using a cookie cutter or sharp knife, cut out star shapes; lift off using a metal spatula.

6 Transfer the parfait to the refrigerator 30 minutes before serving to let it soften. Just before serving, stick the chocolate stars into the top of the parfait and dust lightly with sifted confectioners' sugar.

Iced orange parfaits with citrus sauce

If you don't have individual molds, freeze the parfait in a bread pan and serve cut into slices.

Makes 6

for the parfait
3 oranges
1/2 lemon
3 egg yolks
1/2 cup superfine sugar
1 tbsp. orange-flavored liqueur
3/4 cup plus 2 tbsp. heavy cream
scant 1/2 cup mascarpone cheese

for the citrus sauce
7 oranges
2 tbsp. superfine sugar
juice of 1/2 lemon
2 tsp. cornstarch
splash of orange-flavored liqueur

to decorate
2 1/2 ounces semisweet chocolate
unsweetened cocoa powder for dusting

1 Make the parfait: Scrub one of the oranges and, without peeling it, cut it into chunks. Process in a food processor or blender until finely chopped. Press through a fine strainer. Squeeze in the juice from the remaining oranges and the lemon.

2 In a bowl, beat the egg yolks and sugar until pale and thick. Stir in the fruit juices and transfer to a pan. Cook over low heat, stirring, until thick enough to coat the back of the spoon; do not let it boil or it will separate. Set aside to cool.

3 When the custard is cool, add the orange liqueur. Transfer to an ice-cream machine and churn until semifrozen. Stir the cream into the mascarpone. Return to the machine and churn until frozen. Spoon the mixture into six 1/2-cup molds or ramekins. Freeze at least 2 hours.

4 Make the sauce: Pare the peel from 2 oranges and cut into matchstick strips. Squeeze the juice from these oranges into a small pan and add the peel. Add the sugar and lemon juice. Simmer 5 minutes until the sugar dissolves and the peel is tender. In a cup, blend the cornstarch with 1 tablespoon water and 1 tablespoon hot juice. Add to the pan and simmer, stirring, 1 minute until the sauce thickens slightly. Add a splash of liqueur; leave to cool.

5 Peel the remaining oranges, removing the pith. Working over a bowl to catch the juice, cut the oranges into segments. Add the juice and segments to the sauce. Cover with plastic wrap; chill.

6 Make the decorations: Line a tray with waxed paper. Melt the chocolate in a heatproof bowl set over a pan of simmering water. Spoon into a small paper pastry bag. Pipe shapes on the prepared tray; leave to set. When firm, peel away the paper.

7 Remove the parfaits from the freezer and dip each mold quickly in hot water. Run a knife around the rim and unmold onto a freezerproof tray; return to the freezer.

8 About 30 minutes before serving, transfer the parfaits to the refrigerator to soften. Place one on each serving plate and surround with the sauce. Decorate with chocolate shapes and dust the plates with cocoa.

Variation:
To make parfait without an ice-cream machine, tip the custard, liqueur, cream, and mascarpone into a bowl and beat until smooth. Pour into a shallow freezerproof container and freeze 1 to 2 hours until the edges are just set. Scrape into a bowl and beat again to remove lumps or ice crystals. Return to the container and freeze 1 hour. Beat again. Spoon into the molds and continue with the recipe. The parfait will not be as smooth as when made in an ice-cream machine, but it will still be delightful.

Punch parfait with punch syrup and almond tuiles

Serves 10

6 tea bags
2½ cups boiling water
2½ cups red wine
2½ cups orange juice
juice of 4 lemons
3¼ cups superfine sugar
6 eggs, plus 6 extra yolks
2 tbsp. dark rum
3½ cups whipping cream

for the almond tuiles
1 stick unsalted butter, softened
1¼ cups confectioners' sugar
3 egg whites
¾ cup plus 1 tbsp. all-purpose flour
½ cup slivered almonds

for the punch syrup
¾ cup plus 2 tbsp. red wine
1 cinnamon stick
grated nutmeg
juice of 1 orange
about ¼ cup packed light Barbados sugar

1 Make the parfait: Put the tea bags in a heatproof pitcher. Pour the boiling water over; leave to infuse 3 minutes. Strain into a pan. Add the wine, citrus juices, and 3 cups of the sugar. Bring to a boil, stirring to dissolve the sugar. Lower the heat and reduce to 2½ cups; this will take about 1½ hours. Leave to cool.

2 In a bowl set over a pan of simmering water, beat the eggs, extra egg yolks, and remaining sugar until the mixture is light and leaves a ribbon on the surface when the beaters are lifted. Fold in two-thirds of the reduced liquid and the rum. Remove from the heat.

3 Whip the cream until it just holds its shape. Fold the remaining reduced liquid into the egg mixture, followed by the whipped cream. Pour into a freezerproof container and freeze at least 4 hours, preferably overnight.

4 Make the tuiles: Beat the butter and sugar together until light and fluffy. Stir in the egg whites. Fold in the flour and almonds. Chill until firm.

5 Heat the oven to 350°F and line a baking sheet with nonstick baking parchment. Spread some tuile batter on the sheet in thin 4-inch circles, allowing space around them for them to expand. Bake 5 to 6 minutes until even golden brown.

6 Leave to cool a few minutes on the baking sheet. Using a metal spatula, lift off the tuiles and drape over a rolling pin. When set, remove and leave to cool on a wire rack. Make the remaining tuiles in the same way.

7 Make the punch syrup: Put all the ingredients in a pan and bring to a boil, stirring to dissolve the sugar. Lower the heat and simmer until a light syrup forms. Strain into a pitcher and cool.

8 Put tablespoons of the parfait in tuiles and arrange about 3 each on individual serving plates. Pour a little syrup around to serve.

Semifrozen strawberry bombes

Makes 6

2 tbsp. red-currant jelly
8 ounces strawberries
4 tbsp. fresh orange juice
2 tbsp. superfine sugar
2 ounces amaretti cookies, plus extra
   to serve
2 cups mascarpone or cream
   cheese

1 Line 6 freezerproof cups or ramekins with plastic wrap. Slowly warm the red-currant jelly. Thinly slice 10 even-sized strawberries. Dip each slice into the red-currant jelly and press to the bottom and sides of the cups.
2 Chop or mash the remaining strawberries. Mix with the orange juice and sugar. Place the cookies between 2 sheets of waxed paper and lightly crush with a rolling pin. Fold the strawberry mixture and crushed cookies into the mascarpone or cream cheese.
3 Fill the cups with the strawberry mixture, pressing it down lightly and smoothing the tops. Cover with plastic wrap and freeze for about 4 hours, or overnight, until firm. Transfer from the freezer to the refrigerator 1 hour before serving; the mixture should be softly frozen.
4 Turn the bombes out onto individual serving plates. Peel off the plastic wrap. Serve with amaretti cookies.

Snowball bombe

Serves 8

1 cup fromage blanc
7 tbsp. superfine sugar
6 tbsp. butter, melted
½ cup diced, ready-to-eat dried
  apricots
⅓ cup shelled hazelnuts, toasted and
  chopped
2 tbsp. chopped candied peel
grated peel and juice of 2 oranges
grated peel and juice of 1 lemon
8 trifle sponges or champagne
  cookies
about 2 cups fresh orange juice
2 envelopes unflavored powdered
  gelatin
⅔ cup whipping cream

1 Place the fromage blanc in a bowl. Beat in the sugar. Beat in the butter, a little at a time, until smooth. Stir in the apricots, hazelnuts, candied peel, and grated orange and lemon peel.
2 Cut each trifle sponge into 3 thin slices. Use 3 or 4 slices to line the bottom of a 5-cup freezerproof bowl. Spoon a layer of the fromage blanc mixture on top. Add another layer of sponge and repeat until you end up with a sponge layer on top.
3 Pour the orange and lemon juices into a measuring pitcher and make up to just 2 cups with orange juice. Pour the juice into a pan and heat. Remove from the heat, sprinkle in the gelatin, and stir until it dissolves. Strain slowly over the bowl, helping the juice down the side and between the slices of sponge by pulling the sponge back with a spoon; chill until set.

4 To serve, dip the bowl quickly in hot water. Unmold onto a serving plate. Beat the cream until thick and use to frost the bombe. Chill until ready to serve.

Variation:

Instead of the dried apricots, use seedless raisins or golden raisins that have been plumped up in orange juice or orange-flavored liqueur.

Passionate orange bombe surprise

As you slice into the dome of sharp citrus and passion fruit, a surprise mass of grated chocolate tumbles out.

Serves 8

juice of 1 lemon
scant ⅔ cup fresh orange juice
2 extra-large egg whites
pinch of salt
¾ cup plus 2 tbsp. sugar
1 tsp. unflavored powdered gelatin
4 passion fruit
1¼ cups whipping cream
7 ounces semisweet chocolate
Cape gooseberries, to decorate

1 Strain the lemon juice into a measuring pitcher. Strain in enough orange juice to make up to ⅔ cup. Beat the egg whites and salt until they hold peaks.
2 Pour the citrus juice into a pan, add the sugar and gelatin and heat slowly until both dissolve. Increase the heat and boil rapidly exactly 3 minutes.
3 Pour the citrus juice in a thin stream onto the egg whites, beating all the time at high speed. Continue beating for several minutes until cool and thick.
4 Halve the passion fruit. Scrape the flesh and seeds onto the egg-white mixture; beat until smooth. Beat the cream until thick but not stiff. Using a rubber spatula, fold into the egg-white mixture.

5 Transfer to a 5-cup metal bombe mold or freezerproof bowl. Spread the mixture up the sides with a slight dip in the middle. Freeze at least 5 hours.
6 When the ice cream is firm, coarsely grate the chocolate. Scoop out the center of the ice cream; set aside. Spoon the chocolate into the cavity until completely filled. Stir the reserved ice cream to soften it and spread it over the chocolate. Freeze again at least 1 hour.
7 Dip the mold quickly in very hot water. Loosen the top edges with a round-bladed knife and unmold onto a freezerproof plate. Return to the freezer until ready to serve. Decorate with Cape gooseberries and serve immediately.

Strawberry Alaska

Serves 8

1 quantity Strawberry Ice Cream (see page 144), or 3 cups premium strawberry ice cream

2 tsp. confectioners' sugar

strawberries, to decorate

for the cake

butter, for greasing

2 eggs

1¼ cups superfine sugar

⅓ cup all-purpose flour

for the meringue

4 egg whites

¾ cup plus 2 tbsp. superfine sugar

1 Line a 7-inch freezerproof bowl with 2 sheets of plastic wrap so the plastic overlaps the edges. Fill the bowl with ice cream and press to make a solid dome shape; fold over the plastic to cover the top. Freeze at least 1 hour.

2 Make the cake: Heat the oven to 425°F. Butter an 8-inch round cake pan and line the bottom with nonstick baking paper. Using an electric mixer, beat the eggs and sugar until double in volume and the mixture leaves a trail on the surface when the beaters are lifted (about 5 minutes).

3 Sift the flour over. Using a large metal spoon, fold it into the egg mixture. Spoon into the cake pan and lightly spread it to the edges. Bake 8 minutes until pale golden and springy to the touch. Leave to cool in the pan 5 minutes. Unmold, remove the paper, and leave to cool completely on a wire rack. (Keep the oven on for the meringue.)

4 Make the meringue: In a clean, greasefree bowl, beat the egg whites until soft peaks form. Add 1 tablespoon of the sugar and beat again until stiff. Using a large metal spoon, fold in the rest of the sugar, trying not to knock out any of the air.

5 Place the cooled cake on a lightly greased baking sheet or flameproof plate. Invert the ice-cream dome on the middle of the cake; discard the plastic wrap. Using a tablespoon, cover the ice cream and cake with the meringue, swirling it in patterns. Dust with sifted confectioners' sugar.

6 Bake 6 minutes until the meringue is set and tinged golden brown.

7 Serve immediately, with a few strawberries for decoration.

Quick-baked Alaskas

This dessert is really quick and easy to make. The trick is to make sure the ice cream is firmly frozen.

Makes 6

1¼ cups Strawberry Ice Cream (see page 144)

3 tbsp. superfine sugar

pinch cream of tartar

4 large egg whites

1 tbsp. drinking chocolate powder

1 Heat the oven to 450°F. Pack the ice cream into six ⅔-cup ramekins. Place in the freezer 15 to 20 minutes until firm.

2 Meanwhile, mix together the sugar and cream of tartar. In a separate bowl, beat the egg whites until stiff. Still beating, add the sugar mixture to the egg, a little at a time, until stiff, glossy peaks form.

3 Remove the ramekins from the freezer. Quickly spoon the meringue on top of the ice cream. Place in the oven and bake 4 to 5 minutes until the meringue is browned.

4 Remove from the oven. Dust with the drinking chocolate powder and serve immediately.

Mellow Fruitfulness

A luscious medley of fruit desserts

Figs and clementines poached in port wine

Serves 4

⅔ cup port wine
½ cup granulated sugar
pared peel of 1 lemon
1 cinnamon stick
8 small fresh figs
4 clementines, peeled
to serve
crème fraîche or sour cream
ground cinnamon

1 Place the port, sugar, lemon peel, and cinnamon stick in a pan with ⅔ cup water. Heat slowly, stirring, until the sugar dissolves. Bring to a boil and boil rapidly 3 minutes.
2 Using a knife, open out the figs into 4 segments, or leave them whole, if you prefer. Add to the syrup with the clementines. Cover and poach 6 to 8 minutes until tender. Using a slotted spoon, transfer the fruit to a serving dish.
3 Remove the lemon peel and cinnamon stick

from the syrup; discard them. Bring the syrup to a boil and boil rapidly until reduced by half. Pour over the fruit. Leave to cool, chill.
4 Serve chilled, with crème fraîche dusted with cinnamon.

Pears baked in honey

Serves 6

6 firm pears
6 cloves
8 cardamom seeds, cracked
2 cinnamon sticks
for the honey syrup
2 tbsp. superfine sugar
4 to 6 tbsp. honey

1 Heat the oven to 400°F. Peel the pears, leaving the stalks in place, and remove the cores. Stick a clove in each pear. Lay them on their sides in a baking dish. Scatter the cardamom seeds and cinnamon sticks on top of the pears.
2 Make the honey syrup: Dissolve the sugar and honey in 1¼ to 2 cups boiling water. Pour over the pears; the pears should be half covered in liquid. Bake about 1 hour or until tender, basting

occasionally. Serve hot or let the pears cool in the honey syrup.

Toffee strawberries

Makes 20

vegetable oil, for greasing
1¼ cups superfine sugar
5 tbsp. dextrose
1 pound strawberries

(See the picture on page 154)

1 Cover a baking sheet with foil and oil it lightly. Place a small bowl of cold water and a pastry brush next to the stovetop.
2 Pour ½ cup water into a heavy-bottomed pan. Add the sugar and stir. Simmer on low heat until the sugar dissolves, without stirring.
3 If the sugar bubbles up inside the pan, wash down with the pastry brush dipped in cold water; this prevents crystals from forming. Add the dextrose and lower a candy thermometer into the liquid. Partially cover the pan with a lid and cook over high heat until the temperature reaches

305°F, or until the mixture turns pale golden. Remove from the heat; leave to cool slightly 2 minutes.
4 Stick a wooden skewer or popsicle stick into the green part of the strawberry. Dip and turn the strawberries in the toffee, letting any excess run off. Place the coated strawberries on the foil-covered baking tray; leave to set about 5 minutes.
5 Serve immediately because the toffee will start to dissolve after about 1 hour.

Poached apricots with vanilla syrup

Serves 4

1¾ cups sugar
1 lemon
2 vanilla beans, split in half
24 to 36 dried apricots, soaked
    overnight in cold water and drained
4 tbsp. chilled unsalted butter,
    diced
mascarpone cheese, to serve

1 In a pan, dissolve the sugar in 2½ cups water, stirring occasionally.

2 Pare the peel from the lemon and cut it into thin strips. Squeeze the juice from the lemon into the pan and add the peel. Bring to a boil and boil 1 minute; remove from the heat.

3 Add the vanilla beans to the pan; stir well. Add the apricots and bring to a boil. Lower the heat and simmer 5 minutes.

4 Strain through a fine strainer into a clean pan; set the apricots and vanilla beans aside. Bring the syrup to a boil and boil 2 minutes until it is slightly thick. Increase the heat and gradually beat in the butter. Don't let the syrup get too thick; add a few tablespoons of water, if necessary.

5 Place 6 to 9 apricots on each plate. Top with a piece of vanilla bean, if you like. Spoon the vanilla syrup over.

6 Serve immediately, with spoonfuls of mascarpone.

Poached pears with chocolate sauce

Makes 4

4 firm pears, peeled
4 tbsp. superfine sugar
juice and pared peel of ½ lemon
3½ ounces semisweet chocolate,
    broken into pieces
3 to 4 tbsp. heavy cream

1 Slice the pears in half, leaving the stalks intact. Scoop out the cores. Pour 2 cups water into a skillet. Add the sugar and lemon juice and peel and heat slowly until the sugar dissolves.

2 Bring the liquid to a boil. Add the pear halves and cover with a dampened circle of nonstick baking paper. Simmer 10 minutes, or until the pears are tender when pierced with a knife; leave to cool in the poaching liquid.

3 Place the chocolate in a small pan with 6 tablespoons of the poaching liquid and melt over very low heat, stirring continuously, until smooth; remove from the heat.

4 Divide the chocolate sauce between 4 dessert plates. Spoon little dots of the cream on each plate and feather with the tip of a skewer or toothpick. Remove the pears from the poaching liquid and pat dry with paper towels. Arrange on top of the chocolate sauce. Serve at once.

Caramelized pear brioche with almond custard sauce

Serves 4

4 medium-ripe pears
2 tbsp. unsalted butter
2 tbsp. superfine sugar
1 tbsp. Poire William or brandy
4 thin slices brioche
fresh mint sprigs, to decorate
    (optional)

for the almond custard sauce
2 egg yolks
2 tbsp. superfine sugar
½ cup milk
½ cup light cream
10 blanched almonds, finely ground
few drops almond extract (optional)

1 Quarter the pears, peel, remove the cores, and cut each piece in half.

2 Place the butter and sugar in a skillet. Cook over medium heat a few minutes until caramelized. Carefully pour in ⅔ cup water; bring to a boil.

3 Add the pear slices and cook about 10 minutes over high heat, shaking the pan occasionally, so the pears absorb the syrup. Add the Poire William or brandy and cook 1 to 2 minutes, shaking the pan until the pears are coated in a syrupy glaze.

4 Make the custard sauce: Beat the egg yolks with the sugar until pale. Warm the milk, cream, and almonds until just below a boil. Pour the cream mixture over the egg yolks and stir. Return the custard to the pan and cook over very low heat without boiling, stirring continuously about 15 minutes until thick. Stir in the almond extract, if using.

5 Toast the brioche slices. Serve them topped with the pears and with custard sauce poured around each portion. Decorate with mint sprigs, if you like.

159

Caramel rice and plum compote

In this version of an old-fashioned favorite, a crisp caramel replaces the traditional "skin" of a baked pudding.

Serves 6

for the caramel rice
3¾ cups milk
scant ⅓ cup short-grained pudding rice
½ cup superfine sugar
⅔ cup light cream

for the plum compote
½ cup packed light Barbados sugar
1½ pounds plums, pitted and quartered
1 cinnamon stick, halved
2 bay leaves

1 Put the milk in the pan with the rice and three-quarters of the sugar. Bring to just below a boil. Lower the heat and simmer 20 to 25 minutes until thick and smooth.

2 Meanwhile, make the compote: Put the sugar in a pan with 2 cups water. Heat slowly, stirring, until the sugar dissolves. Bring to a boil and boil 3 minutes. Add the plums, cinnamon, and bay leaves. Cover and simmer over very low heat about 10 minutes until the plums are soft.

3 Stir the cream into the rice. Meanwhile, heat the broiler to medium. Spoon into a 5-cup baking dish that is suitable for serving from. Sprinkle with the remaining sugar. Broil until the sugar lightly caramelizes.

4 Serve warm or chilled with the compote.

Summer soup of red fruits in citrus sauce

There's no reason why you should limit this delicious dessert to summer because you can buy frozen fruit all year long. Just leave to thaw for several hours and drain off the excess juice.

Serves 6

juice of 2 grapefruits
juice of 2 oranges
juice of 2 lemons
2 passion fruits, halved, pulp and seeds scooped out and reserved
1 kiwi fruit, peeled and finely diced
6 strawberries, hulled and finely diced
2 pounds mixed red fruits, such as strawberries, raspberries, and red currants

1 In a large bowl, mix together the citrus juices. Stir in the passion fruit pulp and seeds, the kiwi fruit, and diced strawberries.

2 Arrange the red fruit in the center of 6 serving plates. Spoon the citrus sauce and diced fruit mixture around the red fruits. Serve the "soup" at once.

Rhubarb compote

Orange and ginger or cinnamon are the nicest flavors to combine with rhubarb. They work especially well as a compote.

Serves 4

½ cup sugar
1 cinnamon stick or a few slices of
  fresh ginger
3 cups chopped rhubarb
juice and finely grated peel of 1
  orange
whipped cream to serve

1 Slowly heat 2½ cups water with the sugar and stir until the sugar dissolves.
2 Add the cinnamon stick or ginger. Simmer for a few minutes; check that it has a good flavor. Remove the spices and add the rhubarb. Bring to a simmer, cover, and simmer 2 to 3 minutes until just tender, but not collapsing.
3 Using a slotted spoon, lift out the rhubarb; set aside. Boil the syrup until thick. Stir in the orange juice and peel. Pour over the rhubarb and leave to cool. Chill before serving, topped with whipped cream.

Variations:
* Use lime peel and juice in place of the orange.
* For a delicious combination, toss in fresh sliced strawberries just before serving.

Bottling is an ideal way of storing excess summer fruit. It is most suitable for fruits that do not freeze well, but only bottle those in peak condition.

Spiced pears

Makes about 3¹/₂ cups

2¹/₂ cups superfine sugar
1¹/₄ cups white vinegar
1-inch piece of fresh ginger, sliced
5 whole cloves
1 cinnamon stick
pared peel and juice of 1 lemon
2 pounds pears

1 Place the sugar and vinegar in a preserving pan. Add the ginger, cloves, cinnamon, and lemon peel to the pan. Simmer over a low heat until the sugar dissolves.
2 Peel the pears, halve and core them, or leave them whole if they are small. Rub the pears with a little lemon juice to prevent discoloration. Place the pears in the syrup, cover, and simmer over a low heat until tender.
3 Pack the pears and a few of the spices into sterilized jars. Boil and reduce the syrup by half and pour over the pears so it just covers them,

leaving a ¹/₂-inch space between the fruit and the lid.
4 Leave to cool. Seal and label with the date and its name. Leave 1 month before eating, so the flavors develop more fully.

Variations:
Use the same method to make spiced apricots, peaches, and apples. Or use whole crab apples with their skins on. Cooking times will vary, however.

Bottled cherries

Bottled fruit should be stored in jars with rubber seals and airtight, screwtop lids. To sterilize the jars, use new rubber seals and sterilize them in boiling water 10 minutes.

Makes about 1¹/₂ quarts

1 cup plus 2 tbsp. sugar
3 pounds cherries, stalks intact
5 to 6 tbsp. brandy

1 Place the sugar and 2¹/₂ cups water in a large pan. Bring to a boil. Lower the heat and simmer 4 minutes. Leave to cool; set aside.
2 Trim the stalks to 1 inch and tightly pack whole cherries into sterilized jars. Mix the brandy with the syrup. Pour over the fruit to cover it completely, leaving a ¹/₂-inch space between the fruit and the lid. Seal.
3 Line the base of a large, deep pan or fish kettle with a double layer of paper towels. Stand the jars inside, making sure they do not touch; if in doubt, place more folded paper between them because they may crack if they touch each other during processing.
4 Pour in enough cold water to come just below the neck of the bottles. Replace the pan lid and bring slowly to a boil. Lower the heat and simmer 30 minutes.

5 Remove the jars and set them on a wooden board to cool; do not place on a cool surface or they will crack. Label with the date and its name. These will keep up to 6 months in a cool dark, dry place.

Variations:
* Raspberries or blackberries, or a combination: follow the same method as above.
* Peaches, nectarines, or apricots: leave whole or halve them. Blanch and peel the fruit first. Bottle as above.
* Pears and apples: peel, core, and halve or quarter. Bottle as above.
* Experiment by adding different liqueurs or flavorings to the syrup, such as ¹/₂ vanilla bean, a few crushed cardamom pods, or a cinnamon stick.

Nectarines with pomegranate

This is a refreshing dessert to serve after a rich, spicy, or heavy meal.

Serves 4

1 pomegranate
4 nectarines, pitted and cut into
  wedges
2 large bananas, thickly sliced
1 large pink grapefruit or 2 blood
  oranges, segmented
1¼ cups fresh orange or
  pineapple juice
fancy cookies, to serve (optional)

1 Halve the pomegranate and scoop out the seeds and pulp. Add to a serving bowl with the remaining ingredients. Toss to combine; cover and chill until required.
2 Serve with cookies, if you wish.

Variations:
Add chopped fresh pineapple or diced mango flesh.

Poached peaches with pistachios

The sparkling wine gives a delicate flavor to the peaches, but you can use apple juice if your prefer. For special occasions, add a splash of fruit brandy or liqueur.

Serves 6

8 peaches
1 bottle sparkling wine, or 3 cups
  apple juice
1 vanilla bean
2 red-fruit tea bags
8 ounces raspberries
½ cup shelled pistachio nuts,
  chopped

1 Pack the peaches in a single layer in a pan. Pour the wine or apple juice over and tuck the vanilla bean and the tea bags underneath a peach to prevent them floating to the surface. Cover and bring to a boil. Immediately turn off the heat; leave to cool completely.
2 Remove the vanilla bean and tea bag; discard. Peel and halve the peaches, remove the pits, and slice the flesh.
3 Put the peach slices in a serving dish with the raspberries. Spoon some of the poaching liquid over. Serve the fruit sprinkled with the chopped pistachios.

Spiced fruit salad

Serves 2

2 tbsp. butter
½ tsp. coriander seeds, crushed
6 cardamom pods, lightly crushed
1 tsp. ground ginger
¼ tsp. cumin seeds
½ papaya, cut into slices
½ small pineapple, peeled, cored, and
  cut into wedges
4 Cape gooseberries, papery husk
  turned back
1 lime, cut in half, plus the juice of ½ lime
2 baby bananas, halved
⅓ cup unpacked shredded coconut,
  toasted, to serve (optional)
generous scoop of vanilla ice cream or a
  spoonful of plain yogurt, to serve

1 Melt the butter in a large skillet. Stir in
the coriander, cardamom pods, ginger,
and cumin. Fry 2 to 3 minutes.
2 Place the papaya, pineapple, Cape
gooseberries, and lime, cut side down, in
the spiced butter. Fry 5 to 8 minutes,
turning frequently, until soft and golden.
Add the bananas and cook 2 minutes
longer. Squeeze in the lime juice and cook
1 minute longer.
3 Serve sprinkled with the toasted
coconut, if using, and a generous scoop of
vanilla ice cream or a spoonful of yogurt.

Deep-fried strawberries with black-currant sauce

Makes 4

1 cup black currants, thawed if frozen
1/4 cup superfine sugar
1 tbsp. fresh lemon juice
8 sheets of phyllo pastry dough, each measuring 8 inches square
20 not-too-ripe strawberries
1 to 2 tsp. balsamic vinegar
finely grated peel of 1 lime
confectioners' sugar, for dusting
1 beaten egg, for glazing
vegetable oil, for deep-frying
ground cinnamon, extra strawberries, and mint sprigs (optional), to decorate

1 Make the black-currant sauce: Place the black currants, sugar, and lemon juice in a food processor or blender and process until smooth; add a little water if the sauce is too thick. Strain through a fine strainer into a bowl; set aside.
2 Lay one sheet of phyllo pastry dough on the work surface. Place another on top at a different angle to make a star shape. Place five strawberries in the middle of each star. Sprinkle over a little balsamic vinegar and one-quarter of the lime peel. Dust with sifted confectioners' sugar to taste. Brush the edges of the dough with egg. Bring up the edges and crimp together at the top to seal. Repeat to make three more bundles.

3 Heat the oil to 300°F in a deep, heavy-bottomed pan or wok. Fry the bundles, one at a time, about 4 minutes each until golden brown. Remove with a slotted spoon and drain on paper towels.
4 Spoon some black-currant sauce into the center of 4 serving plates. Place a phyllo bundle in the middle. Dust with sifted confectioners' sugar and cinnamon, and decorate with strawberries and mint sprigs, if you like.

Lemon, chocolate, and berry roulade

Serves 8

oil, for greasing
4 large eggs
1/2 cup plus 2 tbsp. sugar, plus extra for sprinkling
1/2 tsp. vanilla extract
2/3 cup unpacked shredded coconut
grated peel and juice of 1 lemon
6 ounces semisweet chocolate
1 1/4 cups heavy cream, whipped
8 ounces mixed berries, such as red currants, raspberries, and strawberries, stalks removed, hulled, and halved, if necessary
fresh mint and extra berries, to decorate
confectioners' sugar, for dusting

1 Heat the oven to 400°F. Lightly grease a 13 x 9-inch jelly-roll pan and line with waxed paper.
2 Using an electric mixer, beat the eggs, sugar, and vanilla 5 minutes until thick and frothy and the beaters leave a trail on the surface when lifted. Fold in the coconut and lemon peel. Pour into the prepared pan and smooth the surface.
3 Bake 12 to 15 minutes until firm; leave to cool on a wire rack.
4 Lay a sheet of waxed paper the same size as the jelly-roll pan on the countertop and sprinkle with the extra sugar. Turn the roulade onto the paper and peel off the lining paper. Trim the edges of the roulade. Sprinkle the lemon juice over.
5 Melt the chocolate in a heatproof bowl set over a pan of simmering water. Spread it over the roulade; leave to cool slightly. Spread two-thirds of the cream over the roulade and top with the fresh berries. Lift the paper along one of the short

sides and use to help roll up the roulade.
6 Decorate with the reserved cream, extra fresh berries, and mint sprigs. Dust with sifted confectioners' sugar to serve.

Fruit tuile baskets with sabayon

Makes 8

for the tuile baskets
2 large egg whites
½ cup superfine sugar
1½ tbsp. all-purpose flour
1 cup chopped roasted hazelnuts
4 tsp. hazelnut oil
1 large, firm orange
1 pound mixed red fruit, such as red
   currants, raspberries, and
   strawberries, stalks removed, hulled,
   and sliced, if necessary
confectioners' sugar, for dusting

for the sabayon
2 large egg yolks
3 tbsp. superfine sugar
4 tbsp. sweet white wine

1 Make the tuiles: Heat the oven to 400°F. Cut out eight 8-inch squares of nonstick baking paper and draw a 5-inch circle in the center of each. Divide between 2 baking sheets.
2 Beat the egg whites in a small bowl with a fork until frothy. Stir in the superfine sugar, flour, hazelnuts, and hazelnut oil. Put one-eighth of the mixture on each circle and spread evenly to the edges of the circles. Bake 5 to 8 minutes.
3 Quickly lift off the baking paper and shape into baskets using the orange as a mold; if the tuiles set hard before you shape them, return to the oven for a couple of minutes until soft and repeat the process. Leave to cool on wire racks. When completely cool, arrange the fruit in the baskets.
4 To make the sabayon, place the egg yolks, superfine sugar, wine, and 2 tablespoons water in a large, heatproof bowl over a pan of simmering water. Using an electric mixer, beat 7 to 8 minutes until thick and frothy.
5 Dust the fruit baskets with sifted confectioners' sugar. Serve with the sabayon sauce.

Exotic fruit brûlée

Serves 6 to 8

a selection of exotic fruit, such as
   passion fruit, mango, persimmon,
   papaya, and star fruit
juice of 1 lime
6 tbsp. superfine sugar
1¼ cups heavy cream
1¼ cups thick plain yogurt
¼ cup granulated sugar

1 Halve the passion fruit and scoop out the seeds. Peel the mango, persimmon, and papaya, and chop the flesh into small pieces. Slice the star fruit. Mix all fruit with the lime juice and 2 tablespoons of the sugar.
2 Put the fruit into the bottom of a shallow flameproof dish suitable for serving from. Whip the cream until stiff. Fold in the yogurt and the remaining sugar. Spread evenly over the fruit, making sure it is completely covered. Smooth the top; chill 2 hours.

3 Heat the broiler. Sprinkle the granulated sugar evenly over the cream. Place under the broiler until browned, turning it as necessary.
4 Serve immediately or chill up to 4 hours.

Variation:
This is equally delicious using a selection of summer berries. Replace the lime juice with lemon or orange juice and add grated peel from the fruit to the cream for the topping.

Fleet of Fruit

Fruit tempura

Serves 4

Beat together ⅔ cup self-rising flour, 1 teaspoon ground cinnamon, and ¾ cup plus 2 tablespoons sparkling mineral water to make a smooth batter. Dip ½ pound halved strawberries, two diagonally sliced bananas, and wedges of two peaches into the batter; shake off excess. Shallow-fry in hot vegetable oil 2 to 3 minutes on each side until golden. Drain on paper towels. Serve hot, lightly dusted with sifted confectioners' sugar.

Griddled peaches on toast

Serves 2

Brush a griddle pan with butter. Fry 2 sliced peaches or 4 sliced apricots 2 to 3 minutes on each side. Toast 4 slices of fruit bread. Combine 2 tablespoons butter, 1 tablespoon superfine sugar, and ½ teaspoon ground cinnamon; spread over the toast. Top with warm fruit and a dollop of whipped cream.

Peppered melon and raspberry salad

Serves 4

Mix the cubed flesh of one small melon, ½ pound raspberries, the juice of 1 orange, and 2 tablespoons chopped fresh mint; chill. Top with ground black pepper and decorate with mint sprigs.

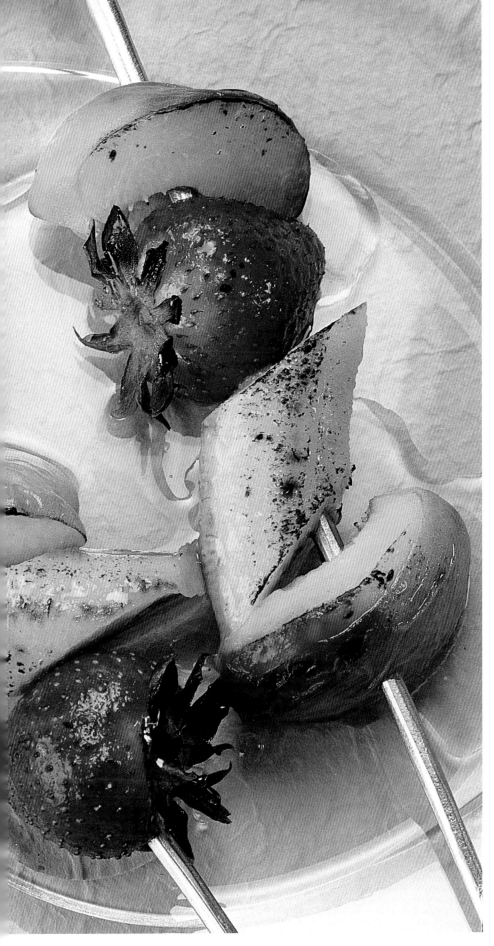

Fruit kabobs

Spear whole strawberries and slices of peach and banana on skewers. Brush with melted butter and barbecue or broil 5 minutes, turning frequently, until lightly browned. Drizzle with a little honey or maple syrup. Serve warm.

Raspberry and ginger oat crunch

Serves 4

Divide 4 ounces raspberries between 4 wine glasses. Stir together 2¼ cups thick plain yogurt, 2 pieces of finely chopped preserved ginger, and 2 tablespoons of the ginger syrup. Spoon over the fruit. Chill, then top each with 2 tablespoons of crunchy oat cereal. Serve at once.

Acknowledgments

Most of the recipes in this book first appeared in *Good Food* or *Vegetarian Good Food* magazine. We are indebted to all those staff (past and present) involved in both magazines, and would especially like to thank Mary Cadogan for providing so many of the recipes.

Recipes by

Nadine Abensur
Plum, apricot, and almond tart p88

Tom Aiken, Chef
Pear crisps p36, from the restaurant, Pied à Terre, Charlotte Street, London

Michael Barry
Breakfast pancakes p61, Pears baked in honey p157

Valerie Berry
Buttermilk pancakes with apple, pecan, and maple syrup p62

Angela Boggiano
Fruit Pavlova p22, Hazelnut, banana, and caramel nests p28, Saffron meringues with lemon syllabub p29, Exotic fruit layer p29, Pear and almond tatin p83, Orange marmalade steamed pudding p130, Individual chocolate and hazelnut puddings p133, Ginger, lemon, and honey steamed pudding p133, Pear and almond steamed pudding p134

Angela Boggiano & Silvana Franco
Mascarpone and rum trifle p36, Crunchy cappuccino ice cream p142

Lorna Brash
Mississippi meringue pie p27, Waffles with date and orange compote p62, Lemon, chocolate, and berry roulade p166, Fruit tuile baskets with sabayon p168

Lorna Brash & Sue Townsend Clark
Peach and honeycomb fools p46, Almond palmiers with nectarine cream p46, Nectarines with pomegranate p164, Poached peaches with pistachios p164

Nicholas Bray, Junior Masterchef
Mille-feuille of raspberries and Florentine cookies p94 © Union Pictures Ltd

Orla Broderick
Meringue peaches p24, Summer fruit sabayon p48, Lemon crêpes p61, Mixed berry pie p75, Satsuma and raisin pie p75, French apple tart p76, Tropical mango tart p80, Paris-Brest p90,

Chocolate roulade p102, Brown bread pudding p125, Peach popovers p128, Poached pears with chocolate sauce p158

Sara Buenfeld
Coconut cream with Malibu fruits p47, White chocolate and blueberry cheesecake p51, Chocolate puddings with white chocolate and Amaretto sauce p108

Mary Cadogan
Apple soufflés p11, Hot lemon soufflés p11, Chocolate praline soufflé with marinated berries p12, Dark mocha soufflés with ice cream and mocha sauce p12, Nectarine mousse cake p18, White and dark chocolate mousse p20, Meringue Christmas tree p30, Red currant meringue roulade p30, Hazelnut meringue roulade with mango and orange cream p33, Raspberry syllabub trifle p38, Currants in red-wine molds p51, Crêpes Suzettes p58, Yorkshire curd tart p68, Pear crumble tart p71, Oranges and lemons basket p76, Smooth butterscotch tart p89, White chocolate puffs filled with lemon cream p92, Mincemeat and apple strudel p96, Apple and pecan phyllo pie p97, Zuccotto p111, Lemon and almond cake p116, Raisin and vanilla cheesecake p123, New Orleans bread pudding with bourbon sauce p124, Almond and orange baked apples p128, Gingered fruit steamed pudding p134, Apricot, pecan, and pear steamed pudding p135, Apple flapjack steamed pudding p137, Frozen peach yogurt p145, Peach melba swirl p145, Chocolate and chestnut parfait p147, Semifrozen strawberry bombes p150, Exotic fruit brûlée p168

R. Chamberlain (reader)
Double-choc mud pie p113

Jacqueline Clarke
Basic crêpes p54, Orange crêpes with spiced fruit compote p56

Ailsa Cruickshank
Pear and kumquat tart p73, Christmas ice cream p143, Figs and clementines poached in port wine p157

Gilly Cubitt
Caramelized banana tarts with vanilla custard sauce p74, Pineapple puddings p119

Josceline Dimbleby
Apricot, rosemary, and honey mousse p18, Fudge apples with orange layered top p119, Snowball bombe p151, Passionate orange bombe surprise p151

Lewis Esson
Apple and cinnamon sugar crêpes p57, Tarte tatin p82, Quick apricot and pine nut tatin p82, Orange-chocolate cheesecake p123, Baked apples p127, Atholl brose ice cream p143

Joanna Farrow
Strawberry mousses p20, Chocolate marquise slice p21, Passion fruit islands p24, Cherry and almond queen of puddings p27, Orange cheesecake brûlée with orange sauce, Instant fruit brûlée p43, Light lemon and nutmeg brûlées p44, Chocolate-praline brûlées p45, Treacle tart p84, Amaretti and almond torte p87, Chocolate indulgence p93, Brandy snaps with chocolate cream p94, Chocolate brownie cake p100, Mocha roulade p104, Lemon and lime pudding p118, Caramel rice and plum compote p160

Ursula Ferrigno
Almond and pear tart p66, Fig and lemon tart p66, Chocolate tart p104

Silvana Franco
Fruit tempura p170, Griddled peaches on toast p170, Peppered melon and raspberry salad p170, Fruit kabobs, Raspberry and ginger oat crunch p171

Linda Fraser
Rhubarb compote p161

Jan Fullwood
Spiced fruit salad p165

Shirley Gill
Apricot and pecan cheesecakes p120

The Good Food Team
Spangled berry cream p48, Quick apricot fool p49, Profiteroles with chocolate sauce p92, Apricot-almond shortcake p116

Peter Gorton, Head Chef
Dark chocolate mousse in a spiced tuile basket p17 from his restaurant, The Horn of Plenty, Devon

Kevin Graham
Louisiana bread pudding p125

Masayuki Hara
Roasted pear bundles with ginger and caramel sauce p126

Ainsley Harriott
Banoffee tart p113, from his book, *In the Kitchen with Ainsley Harriott* (BBC Books)

Petra Jackson
Lacy peach crêpes p57, Phyllo apple strudels p97

Sybil Kapoor
Cranberry and almond tart p79

Sue Lawrence
Seven-cup steamed pudding with a butterscotch sauce p137, from her book, *Entertaining at Home in Scotland*

Jane Lawrie
Cappuccino cups p112, Magic chocolate pudding p112

Gill MacLennan
White chocolate cheesecake p107, Moist chocolate-banana loaf p107, White freezer cake with sticky brownie base p109

John McQ
Quick-baked Alaskas p152

Maggie Mayhew
Blueberry and cranberry tartlets p78

Angela Nilsen
Sour-cream and apple crumb pie p79, Sweet potato pie with toffee pecans p84, Glossy chocolate and peanut butter pie p87, Vanilla ice cream p140

Ian Parmenter
Peach clafoutis p129

Louise Pickford
Baked stuffed pears p127

Gary Rhodes
Chilled Valentine's mousses p17, Rhubarb and white chocolate trifle p38, Lemon crème brûlée with roasted peaches p40, Griddled strawberries with lemon curd ice cream and lemon shortbread p146

Michel Roux
Candied fruit soufflés p14, from his book, *Desserts* (Conran Octopus)

Bridget Sargeson
Raspberry sorbet in strawberry tuiles with dried strawberry slices p144, Strawberry Alaska p152, Toffee strawberries p157

Bill Sewell
Lemon and almond tart p72, from his book, *Food from the Place Below* (HarperCollins)

Jane Suthering
Chocolate brownies p100, Caramelized pear brioche with almond custard sauce p159

Brigitte Tilleray
Tarte aux groseilles meringuée p33

Linda Tubby
Blue cheese, pear, and pecan puffs p80

Phil Vickery
Lace crêpes with raspberries and honey cream p56, Bitter chocolate tart with coffee-bean syrup p71, Bitter chocolate puddings with chocolate fudge sauce p111, Punch parfait with punch syrup and almond tuiles p149, Poached apricots with vanilla syrup p158, Deep-fried strawberries with black-currant sauce p166

Mandy Wagstaff
Baked blueberry cheesecake p122, Strawberry ice cream p144, Frozen strawberry yogurt terrine p147, Iced orange parfaits with citrus sauce p148, Spiced pears p163, Bottled cherries p163

Tony Weston
Highland flummery p49, from his restaurant, The Taigh na Mara Vegetarian Guesthouse, Ullapool

Jenny White
Cranberry, pear, and chocolate trifle (with pear crisps) p36, Fig and marsala trifles p37, Quick rhubarb tarts p81, Fruity baked cheesecake p120

David Wilson
Summer soup of red fruits in citrus sauce p160, from his restaurant, The Peat Inn, Fife

Mitzie Wilson
Tiramisu cheesecake p44

Photographers

Marie-Louise Avery
Iced orange parfaits with citrus sauce p148

Steve Baxter
Magic chocolate pudding p112, Apricot almond shortcake p117

Martin Brigdale
Michel Roux's sauces (detail) p1, Exotic fruit layer p4 & p8, Lemon crêpes p4 & p52, Fruit Pavlova (detail) p9, Apple soufflé p10, Dark mocha soufflés with ice cream and mocha sauce p13, Making a soufflé step-by-steps p14, Candied fruit soufflé (detail) p14, Candied fruit soufflé p15, Chilled Valentine's mousse p16, Pavlova step-by-steps & detail p22, Fruit Pavlova p23, Hazel, banana, and caramel nests p28, Michel Roux's sauces (detail) p35, Lemon crème brûlée with roasted peaches (detail) p40, Lemon crème brûlée with roasted peaches p41, Tiramisu cheesecake p44, Summer fruit sabayon p48, Quick apricot fool p48,

Highland flummery p49, Bitter chocolate tart with coffee-bean syrup p70, Pear and almond tatin p83, White chocolate cheesecake p106, White freezer cake with stick brownie base p109, Fudge apples with orange layered top p119, Roasted pear bundles with ginger and caramel sauce p126, Baked apples p127, Steamed puddings step-by-steps & detail p130, Orange marmalade steamed pudding p131, Individual chocolate and hazelnut steamed puddings, Ginger, lemon, and honey steamed pudding, Pear and almond steamed pudding p132, Ice cream step-by-steps p140, Vanilla ice cream with pear crisps (detail) p140, Vanilla ice cream with pear crisps p141, Poached apricots with vanilla syrup p158, Caramelized pear brioche with almond custard sauce p159, Deep-fried strawberries with black-currant sauce p167, Fruit tempura p170, Griddled peaches on toast p170, Peppered melon and raspberry salad p170, Fruit kabobs p171, Raspberry and ginger oat crunch p171

Linda Burgess
Baked blueberry cheesecake p122

Peter Cassidy
Coconut cream with Malibu fruits p47, Punch parfait with punch syrup and almond tuiles p149

Polly Farquharson
Raspberry syllabub trifle p38

Ken Field
Spangled berry cream p48, Cranberry and almond tart p79, Plum, apricot, and almond tart p88, Rhubarb compote p161

Gus Filgate
Passion fruit islands p25, Meringue Christmas tree p31, White chocolate and blueberry cheesecake p51, Lace crêpes with raspberries and honey cream p56, Lemon and almond tart p72, Pear and kumquat tart p73, Treacle tart p84, Chocolate puddings with white chocolate and Amaretto sauce p108, Lemon and lime pudding (detail) p115, Lemon and lime pudding p118, New Orleans bread pudding with bourbon sauce p124, Almond and orange baked apples p128, Crunchy cappuccino ice cream p142, Christmas ice cream p143, Figs and clementines poached in port wine p156, Spiced pears p162, Bottled cherries p162, Exotic fruit brûlée p169

Christine Hanscomb
Cranberry, pear, and chocolate trifle with pear crisps p4 & p34, Fig and marsala trifles p37

Alex Hansen
Dark chocolate mousse in a spiced tuile basket p16

David Jordan
Peach and honeycomb fools p46, Almond palmiers with nectarine cream p46, Caramelized banana tarts with vanilla custard sauce p74, Nectarines with pomegranate p164, Poached peaches with pistachios p164, Spiced fruit salad p165

Graham Kirk
Mixed berry pie p75

Jess Koppel
Chocolate brownie cake p5 & p98, Lemon and almond cake p5 & p114, Hot lemon soufflés p11, Chocolate marquise slice p21, Mississippi meringue pie p26, Currants in red-wine molds p50, Lacy peach crêpes p57, Chocolate indulgence p93, Brandy snaps with chocolate cream p95, Chocolate brownie cake (detail) p99, Lemon, chocolate, and berry roulade p166, Fruit tuile baskets with sabayon p168

William Lingwood
Toffee strawberries pp2–3, p5, p154, & (detail) p155, Raspberry sorbet in strawberry tuiles with dried strawberry slices p5, p138 & (detail) p139, Banoffee pie p113, Quick-baked Alaskas p152, Strawberry Alaska p153

Paul Moon
Crêpes à l'orange (detail) p58, Double-choc mud pie p113

James Murphy
Nectarine mousse cake p19, French apple tart p77, Sweet potato pie with toffee pecans p85, Glossy chocolate and peanut butter pie p86, Mincemeat and apple strudel p96, Roulade step-by-steps & detail p102, Chocolate roulade p103, Frozen peach yogurt p145, Semifrozen strawberry bombes p150

Alan Newnham
Breakfast pancakes p60

Thomas Odulate
Waffles with date and orange compote p63

Ian O'Leary
Satsuma and raisin pie p75, Cappuccino cups p112

Nick Pope
Amaretti and almond torte p87

William Reavell
Quick rhubarb tarts p81

Roger Stowell
Bitter chocolate puddings with chocolate fudge sauce p6, Rhubarb and white chocolate trifle p39, Making cheesecake step-by-steps & detail p68, Yorkshire curd tart p69, Blueberry and cranberry tartlets p78, Tropical mango tart p80, Pear and walnut slices p81, Cream-puff dough step-by-steps & detail p90, Paris-Brest p91, Mille-feuille of raspberries and Florentine cookies p94, Bitter chocolate puddings with chocolate fudge sauce p110, Fruity baked cheesecake p121, Peach popovers p128, Gingered fruit steamed pudding p134, Apricot, pecan, and pear steamed pudding p135, Apple flapjack steamed pudding p136, Griddled strawberries with lemon curd ice cream and lemon shortbread p146

Kulbir Thandi
Peach clafoutis p129

Martin Thompson
Hazelnut meringue roulade with mango and orange cream p32, Crème brûlée step-by-steps p40, Orange cheesecake brûlée with orange sauce p42, Chocolate-praline brûlées p45, Crêpes step-by-step no3 & detail p54, Basic crêpes p55, Crêpes Suzettes step-by-steps p58, Crêpes Suzettes p59

Jerry Tubby
Summer soup of red fruits in citrus sauce p160

Struan Wallace
Meringue peaches p24

Philip Webb
Almond and pear tart p4, p64, & (detail) p65, Fig and lemon tart p67, Blue cheese, pear, and pecan puffs p80, Chocolate brownies p101, Mocha roulade p105

Frank Wieder
Louisiana bread pudding p125

Simon Wheeler
Smooth butterscotch tart p89

Huw Williams
Crêpes step-by-steps (detail) p53, Crêpes step-by-steps p54

While every effort has been made to trace and acknowledge all copyright holders, we would like to apologize should there be any errors or omissions.

Index